Sincerest
(mechanically-printed)
personal greetings
from

Ashleigh
Brilliant

I Try To Take One Day at a Time, But Sometimes Several Days Attack Me at Once.

More
BRILLIANT THOUGHTS®
Than Ever

By Ashleigh Brilliant

Creator of Pot-Shots® and Author of
I May Not Be Totally Perfect, but Parts of Me Are Excellent

Woodbridge Press/Santa Barbara, California

Published by

Woodbridge Press Publishing Company
Post Office Box 6189
Santa Barbara, California 93160

Distributed simultaneously in the United States and Canada

Printed in the United States of America

Library of Congress Cataloging in Publication Data

Brilliant, Ashleigh, 1933–
  I Try To Take One Day at a Time, but Sometimes
    Several Days Attack Me at Once.

  Bibliography: p.
  1. Epigrams, American.   I. Title
PN 6281.B647   818'.5402   87-23145
ISBN 0-88007-161-3
ISBN 0-88007-162-1 (pbk.)

Dedication

*This book is dedicated
to the proposition that
all Pot-Shots are created
by Ashleigh Brilliant,
that they are endowed by their creator
with his signature and copyright notice,
and that unauthorized copying
of, by, or for anyone else
shall perish from the earth
as soon as possible.*

Contents

Pot-Shots *BY* **ASHLEIGH BRILLIANT**

© ASHLEIGH BRILLIANT 1979.   POT-SHOTS NO. 1520.

I TRY TO TAKE
ONE DAY AT A TIME,

BUT SOMETIMES
SEVERAL DAYS
ATTACK ME
AT ONCE.

Ashleigh Brilliant

Introduction—
The Life of Your Time

Year We Go Again

This is not really the beginning. Or, if it is, I'm not sure what it's the beginning of. Certainly not of my life; nor (I presume) of yours. Not of my literary career, which (like my life) has already been lurching onward for some time. Not even of this book (at least, not for me), since this introductory part is being written last.

Just possibly it IS the beginning of our relationship, in which case, and however it happened, please consider yourself warmly greeted, and encouraged to stay. If you happen to be on a return visit to this book, everything here is just where you left it. But if you are coming from any or all of my five previous collections of Brilliant Thoughts (known also as Pot-Shots), you are in for some (I hope pleasant) surprises.

Like its predecessors, this book has twelve chapters. But, at some inspired moment, it occurred to me that those divisions could also represent the twelve months of the year. Thus was born the idea of making this particular volume into some kind of calendar or diary, with every day of the year having its own Brilliant Thought and a space for you to write your own daily thoughts, or for any other use you choose.

The trouble with ordinary calendars, however, is that (forgive the expression) they soon become dated. They provide information which applies to only one particular year, and usually to only one particular part of the world. I wanted mine to be a calendar which could be started at any time, in any year, and which would be equally useful (or useless) to anyone anywhere in the world. This was easily achieved simply by leaving off, among other things, the days of the week (which, however, you are, of course, perfectly free to write in for yourself). You will also find, as if to further emphasize that this is not one of those common "annual" calendars, that its year does not start where theirs usually do, and that it ends with a day which, more often than not (at least in three years out of four), theirs don't give you at all.

The Daze Go By

I myself have kept a daily dairy for most of my life, besides retaining other voluminous accumulations of personal writings, records, and other relics. And if only I had another life (or the hereby-solicited voluntary services of some devoted scholar) to index, annotate, edit, and make available all those precious papers in some coherent form, they might be of real interest, and possibly some actual practical value, to somebody somewhere—perhaps even to me.

But even if you never use the spaces provided for each day herein, you need feel no guilt. Nothing has been sacrificed to secure them for you. The same amount of blank space was there in my previous published collections, but was just going to waste. And, thanks to there being so many days in a year, you are, in addition, actually getting substantially more Pot-Shots this time than have ever appeared in one book before.

Even so, it might be best (though I don't insist upon it) if you could ration yourself to just one Pot-Shot per day. The Brilliant epigram (never, under my strict rules, longer than 17 words, and carefully constructed to carry the most weight for the least freight), is a potent verbal vitamin, and can be very beneficial if consumed on a one-a-day basis, as readers of my syndicated newspaper feature continue to inform me. Taking too many at one time, however, can produce severe stupefaction, and, in extreme cases, total paralysis of the mental muscles.

In assigning a Brilliant Thought to each day of the year, I make no clairvoyant claims—although part of the fun I hope to generate lies in the possibility that you will, at least occasionally, find a message amazingly appropriate for its particular day. It may even become fashionable for people meeting at parties to ask each other what Pot-Shot they were born under. But if, for any reason, you don't like the thought attached here to your birthday, I'll be glad to share mine with you (see December 9).

Speaking of birthdays, this whole idea of an any-time any-place diary opens up vast possibilities, and I would very much like to hear from you about how, when, and where you are using it, particularly, (and as a special treat for the occasion), if the time happens to be sometime around my own hundredth birthday, in the year 2033, and even more so if the place is somewhere beyond the Earth.

Marking Time

Whatever the circumstances, between these covers we are going to be spending a year together—a calendar year, divided into months and days. But let's not take this too seriously. The fact that most people, in a world in which so much still separates us, now at least use the same calendar for most purposes, does seem to indicate some kind of progress. But never forget that our whole system of reckoning time is only a game, and that the rules can be changed whenever anybody with sufficient clout lays down the law. The last person to attempt any significant improvement, and make it stick, was Pope Gregory XIII, in 1582, which is why our current system (still imperfect, although the publication of this book now gives me something of a vested interest in it) is called the Gregorian Calendar.

What we call the calendar is, however, of less concern to me, (as you will see), than what we call the months, whose names—all still recognizably persisting in most world languages today—go back to an era of Romans much more bygone than Pope Gregory, and, in four particular cases, incorporate a barefaced misrepresentation which has troubled me ever since I first learned to count in Latin (see Chapters VII, VIII, IX, and X). I ask you to indulge my emphasis upon this matter, since it was (apparently) for this purpose alone that Fate arranged to have me study Latin with special intensity at school in England. My supposed motivation at the time (circa 1950) was to qualify for admission to one of the old prestigious universities, where a knowledge of Latin was then still required. But I didn't get in anyway, so Fate must actually have been looking much farther ahead.

Pot-Shots BY ASHLEIGH BRILLIANT

POT-SHOTS NO. 4199. ©ASHLEIGH BRILLIANT 1987.

WHAT SHALL I DO ABOUT WHO I AM?

Ashleigh Brilliant

Time for Tribute

Another two of our twelve months were actually named for real people (see Chapters V and VI)—a distinction nobody else has been able to attain in the past twenty centuries. My own first name, however, (surely not by pure co-incidence?) has, in recent years, despite some confusion about spelling and gender, actually become one of the most fashionable children's names in America. And, should any such proposal gain momentum, I would have no strong objection to seeing one of the current months renamed Ashleigh—perhaps March, since nowadays who needs a month named for the God of War?

No tribute of that magnitude to my achievements as the world's leading (and perhaps only) professional epigrammatist may yet be at hand, but already the honors and prizes which I have been publicly craving ever since 1967, when I first embarked upon this peculiar career, have begun to shower upon me. If not quite a shower, there has (so far) been at least a single small squirt, in the form of one actual legitimate Award. On April 4, 1987, I received the Raymond B. Bragg Award for Humanism in Entertainment and the Arts. No, I had never heard of it before either, (and in fact this was the first time it had ever been awarded)—but it was worth $2,000, an inscribed plaque, and a free round trip from my home in Santa Barbara to All Souls Unitarian Church in Kansas City, Missouri, where the presentation was made in a formal ceremony. In my acceptance speech, I admitted that I had never considered myself a "humanist," and was not even clear about the meaning of the term—but they let me keep the Award anyway. It was not quite the Nobel Prize for Literature, but at least (I felt) a step closer, and a useful rehearsal.

Only two weeks before this heady occasion, and almost equally momentously, the lofty *Times Literary Supplement* of London had taken formal cognizance of my existence for the first time, with a critique by Mr. Eric Korn extending over two columns.[1] Some of its more favorable comments, adeptly extracted, are proudly exhibited on the back cover of this book. Mr. Korn also pointed out an irony of which I myself have been well aware—that, although the essence of my

[1]*TLS,* March 20, 1987, p. 296.

works is brevity, there are now so many of them (4328 as of this writing, all available on postcards—see fascinating catalogue information, page 163) that they amount to a huge (apparently still unfinished) opus, and lay me open to the aspersion of being "endlessly brief."

Court Calendar

The honor of being widely quoted is also one which continues to bring me some satisfaction, and an increasing part of my income, although the satisfaction (and the income) are somewhat reduced by the constant need to be on guard, and occasionally to take legal action, against copyright infringers. The law, however, is very much on my side, and a U.S. Federal Judge has even been among those who have written to me for permission to quote my work, to enliven some of his decisions. In one case that came before him, the Fuller Brush Company was disputing the right of a former salesman of theirs, who had legally changed his name to Count Fuller, to continue selling door-to-door on his own, wearing wild costumes, and doing an outrageous parody of a Fuller Brush man. The Judge decided in favor of Count Fuller, and in his written decision he quoted my Pot-Shot no. 893, which says, IN AN ORDERLY WORLD, THERE'S ALWAYS A PLACE FOR THE DISORDERLY.[2]

Years, Mine and Hours

But where is all this leading? Count Fuller may have found his place in this world, but my Brilliant Thoughts have not yet found theirs—because their place (surely!) is everywhere. Every achievement simply opens up tantalizing new vistas. One beckoning frontier is the field of translation. After twenty years of their being officially available only in English, the first authorized attempt to bridge the Pot-Shots culture-gap took place on February 9, 1987, with the publication of a bilingual set of my postcards in English and Russian. (This came as a result of my second visit to the Soviet Union, in 1986, during which, having gone there specially prepared to do so, I

[2]Judge Terence T. Evans, *Fuller v. The Fuller Brush Company*, U.S. District Court, Eastern Wisconsin, October 20, 1984.

actually gave several public recitations of selected Pot-Shots, translated into Russian, and found, as expected, that international relations immediately improved.)

New products and adaptations of my work are continually in the offing (although that is frequently where they remain). Even some of my pre-Pot-Shots productions are beginning to receive some tardy acclaim. My Ph.D. dissertation on the Social Effects of the Automobile in Southern California During the 1920's, after languishing in undeserved but total obscurity ever since I wrote it at Berkeley in 1964, somehow resulted, twenty-two years later, in my being unexpectedly sought out and introduced as an "expert" by the National Endowment for the Humanities in a radio series about Los Angeles in the 1920's.[3] My *Haight-Ashbury Songbook,* a luminous celebration of the Hippie Era, was rescued from an almost equally profound oblivion by the strange phenomenon we call nostalgia. Only twenty years had to pass before a San Francisco television station was bringing me back there at its own expense solely to re-enact my original performance of those joyfully subversive songs in Golden Gate Park.[4]

Being so haphazardly lost and found, forgotten and rediscovered, is, I suppose, the inevitable fate of a performing public thinker in a world where there are always so many other shows on the road. But if time can play such pleasant tricks on me, think what it can do for you! So take the very special year I'm about to give you. Don't ask inconvenient questions, such as where I got it, what right I have to give it to you, or what you are supposed to do with it. Just be glad (as I am) that it has found you, and try (please, somehow!) to give it a good home in your life.

[3]"California Times," U.S. Public Radio, 1986.

[4]KGO-TV, "Summer of Love" [20th Anniversary commemoration], May, 1987.

Pot-Shots BY ASHLEIGH BRILLIANT

POT-SHOTS NO. 4147.

YOUR TASK IS SIMPLE:

ELIMINATE
THE DIFFERENCE
BETWEEN
HOW THINGS SHOULD BE
AND
HOW THEY REALLY ARE.

Ashleigh Brilliant

I. March of Time

What! No January or February! Calm down—those months are up ahead, in their proper sequence, and you can begin there (page ＿) if you wish. But I personally have always thought January a terrible time for any year to begin. And so too, apparently, did the earliest ancient Romans, from whom our whole calendar derives, and who began their own ten-month year in March, which they named for their very important god, Mars.

We too celebrate March (and marching) in a special way, by associating them proverbially with Time itself, one of our own most important deities, whose image, in various clock-like forms, we worship throughout our lives, in a strange, but now extremely widespread, species of idolatry.

There is, of course, no real reason to care so much about Time, since evidence is totally lacking that Time cares at all about us. Still, the fact remains that there are 31 days ahead of us which we have decided to call March. And counting this as our first month will enable us, as you will see, to restore four long-dislocated months to their correct numerical places.

Previous Marches have given birth to the telephone (1876) and to Johann Sebastian Bach (1685); and March 17 belongs to Patrick, the patron saint of Ireland, a small country sandwiched uncomfortably between England and America.

Let me also point out (since it might otherwise escape your notice) that March (around the 21st) is the home of one of our two annual equinoxes. With daylight (like so many other good things) usually distributed so unevenly on our planet, I am pleased to tell you that, on this one day in each half-year, everybody, all over the world, gets an exactly equal 12-hour portion. If the thought of sharing so much, at the same time, with so many, excites you, this is clearly a good year's beginning.

POT-SHOTS NO. 4062.

TO WHAT
EXTENT
AM I
CAUSING
MY OWN
UNHAPPINESS?

ISN'T THERE
ANYBODY ELSE
I CAN
LEGITIMATELY
BLAME
FOR IT?

Ashleigh Brilliant
©ASHLEIGH BRILLIANT 1987.

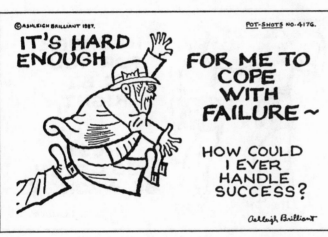

©ASHLEIGH BRILLIANT 1987.

POT-SHOTS NO. 4176.

IT'S HARD ENOUGH

FOR ME TO
COPE
WITH
FAILURE ~

HOW COULD
I EVER
HANDLE
SUCCESS?

Ashleigh Brilliant

©ASHLEIGH BRILLIANT 1987.

POT-SHOTS NO. 4165.

MY MAJOR
HEALTH PROBLEM

IS
SOMETHING
CALLED
BEING
MORTAL.

Ashleigh Brilliant

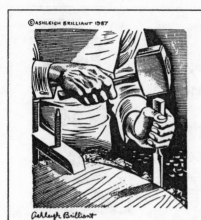

© ASHLEIGH BRILLIANT 1987. POT-SHOTS NO. 4004.

Even with a round table,

some people always seem able to sit at the head of it.

Ashleigh Brilliant

© ASHLEIGH BRILLIANT 1985. POT-SHOTS NO. 3681. Ashleigh Brilliant

DON'T TRY TO CHEER ME UP ~

IT'S ONLY MY STRONG NEGATIVE ATTITUDE THAT KEEPS ME GOING.

POT-SHOTS NO. 4135. Ashleigh Brilliant

THIS IS NOT JUST ANOTHER DAY ~

IT'S THE ONLY ONE YOU'LL HAVE ALL THE WAY UNTIL TOMORROW.

© ASHLEIGH BRILLIANT 1987.

March 16

© ASHLEIGH BRILLIANT 1985.   POT-SHOTS NO. 3365.

I KEEP QUITE BUSY
JUST TRYING
TO CONCEAL
THE FACT
THAT
I DON'T KNOW
WHAT I'M DOING.

Ashleigh Brilliant

March 17

© ASHLEIGH BRILLIANT 1987.   POT-SHOTS NO. 4304.

I WONDER
WHERE
ALL THE
GOOD LUCK
IS
STORED,

AND WHY
ITS RELEASE
AND
DISTRIBUTION
ARE SO
IRREGULAR.

Ashleigh Brilliant

March 18

© ASHLEIGH BRILLIANT 1987.   POT-SHOTS NO. 4066.

WHO CAN
RELEASE ME

FROM MY
SELF-IMPOSED
SENSE OF
OBLIGATION?

Ashleigh Brilliant

© ASHLEIGH BRILLIANT 1985.   POT-SHOTS NO. 3797.

BE CAREFUL HOW YOU
BEHAVE TOWARDS
WILD THINGS ~

REMEMBER
THAT,
TO THEM,
YOU
REPRESENT
CIVILIZATION.

Ashleigh Brilliant

POT-SHOTS NO. 3515.
Ashleigh Brilliant

THE ONLY WAY
YOU CAN GET
TO
HAPPINESS

IS
BY
ALREADY
BEING
THERE.

© ASHLEIGH BRILLIANT 1985.

© ASHLEIGH BRILLIANT 1987.   POT-SHOTS NO. 4312.

NO MATTER
HOW MANY
LIVES
I'M GIVEN,

I THINK
I WOULD
ALWAYS
WANT
ONE
MORE.

Ashleigh Brilliant

March 22

© ASHLEIGH BRILLIANT 1987.　　POT-SHOTS NO. 4087.

THERE'S SUCH A BIG DIFFERENCE

BETWEEN
YOU
AND
NO YOU.

Ashleigh Brilliant

March 23

© ASHLEIGH BRILLIANT 1985　　POT-SHOTS NO. 3556.

TRY TO BELIEVE IN SOMETHING,

BUT, IF YOU BELIEVE IN NOTHING,

AT LEAST DO SO WHOLE-HEARTEDLY.

Ashleigh Brilliant

March 24

© ASHLEIGH BRILLIANT 1985　　POT-SHOTS NO. 3779.

EVERYTHING ABOUT LIFE IS UNBELIEVABLY WONDERFUL,

BUT WE HAVE TO IGNORE THAT,

AND GO ON LIVING ANYWAY.

Ashleigh Brilliant

© ASHLEIGH BRILLIANT 1985   POT-SHOTS NO. 3929.

MENTAL HEALTH
DOESN'T MEAN ALWAYS BEING HAPPY —

IF IT DID, NOBODY WOULD QUALIFY.

Ashleigh Brilliant

© ASHLEIGH BRILLIANT 1987.   POT-SHOTS NO. 4215.

DID YOU EVER REALIZE HOW MUCH PAIN YOU CAUSE ME

BY NOT BEING PERFECT?

Ashleigh Brilliant

© ASHLEIGH BRILLIANT 1987.   POT-SHOTS NO. 4151.

THERE IS NO GOOD OR BAD IN OUTER SPACE

AND WON'T BE UNTIL WE PUT IT THERE.

Ashleigh Brilliant

March 28

TIME PASSES WITH BEWILDERING SPEED,

EXCEPT WHEN I'M WAITING TO SEE YOU.

Ashleigh Brilliant

© ASHLEIGH BRILLIANT 1985.

POT-SHOTS NO. 3584.

March 29

THE HARDEST CREATURES TO TAKE CARE OF

ARE THOSE WHO WANT AND NEED THE LEAST CARE.

© ASHLEIGH BRILLIANT 1985.

POT-SHOTS NO. 3718.
Ashleigh Brilliant

March 30

ONE THING THERE'S NEVER ANY SHORTAGE OF, FOR PEOPLE WHO WANT IT, IS:

RESPONSIBILITY

POT-SHOTS NO. 4155.
Ashleigh Brilliant

© ASHLEIGH BRILLIANT 1987.

II. April Full

Full of what? Whatever you choose (up to a point). For example, if you choose Disasters, I can tell you that the San Francisco Earthquake and Fire (1906), the Loss of the Titanic (1912), and the Chernobyl Nuclear Mishap (1986) all occurred in April. But our friends the Romans were thinking of more pleasant things, such as the buds of their springtime, when they named this month from their word for "opening."

There can, of course, be a connection between disasters and openings, (as any theatrical producer will tell you). But, in celebration of your choosing to spend April with A. Brill., you have my permission to open anything you please during the next 30 days—a bank account, a relationship, or (if you have the proper equipment), even a mind.

Contrary to anything you may have heard, April has nothing to do with apes—except for the traditional activity of making a monkey out of somebody. Somehow, in certain cultures, the idea of foolishness has become attached to the beginning of this month—as if there were any need to encourage idiotic behavior in a world full of politicians and generals. I must, however, admit that one of the funniest of all practical jokes is actually to be born on the first of April—or, for that matter, on any other day of the year.

April 4

POT-SHOTS No. 3902. Ashleigh Brilliant

WHAT
PEOPLE
WON'T DO
FOR
PASSION,

THEY WILL
OFTEN DO
FOR
FASHION.

© ASHLEIGH BRILLIANT 1985.

April 5

Ashleigh Brilliant

POT-SHOTS No. 3952.

I'M
NOT YET
READY FOR
THE FUTURE,

BUT
FORTUNATELY,
IT HASN'T
YET
ARRIVED.

© ASHLEIGH BRILLIANT 1985.

April 6

POT-SHOTS No. 3521.

I NEED
MY HEROES

MORE THAN
I NEED TO KNOW
THE
DISILLUSIONING
TRUTH
ABOUT THEM.

© ASHLEIGH BRILLIANT 1985.

Ashleigh Brilliant

© ASHLEIGH BRILLIANT 1987.

POT-SHOTS NO. 4316.

IT'S HARD FOR INDIVIDUALS TO APOLOGIZE AND FORGIVE EACH OTHER,

BUT SO MUCH HARDER FOR COUNTRIES!

Ashleigh Brilliant

© ASHLEIGH BRILLIANT 1985.

POT-SHOTS NO. 3803.

ONLY ONE THING COMES BETWEEN MANY PARENTS AND THEIR CHILDREN ~

IT'S SOMETHING CALLED FAMILY LIFE.

Ashleigh Brilliant

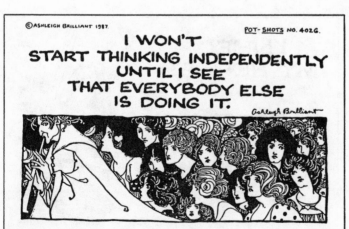

© ASHLEIGH BRILLIANT 1987.

POT-SHOTS NO. 4026.

I WON'T START THINKING INDEPENDENTLY UNTIL I SEE THAT EVERYBODY ELSE IS DOING IT.

Ashleigh Brilliant

April 10

© ASHLEIGH BRILLIANT 1987. POT-SHOTS NO. 4001.

SOMETIMES
THE ONLY WAY
YOU CAN WIN

IS TO
STAY OUT OF
THE GAME.

Ashleigh Brilliant

April 11

© ASHLEIGH BRILLIANT 1985. POT-SHOTS NO. 3691.

REASONABLE PEOPLE
CAN HAVE
REASONABLE
DIFFERENCES
OF OPINION,

SO LONG AS
NOTHING
REALLY IMPORTANT
IS AT STAKE.

Ashleigh Brilliant

April 12

© ASHLEIGH BRILLIANT 1987. POT-SHOTS NO. 4060.

I'VE BEEN
CONSCIOUS
AND
UNCONSCIOUS,

AND I CAN SAY
THIS FOR
UNSCIOUSNESS:

IT
LEAVES
NO
BAD
MEMORIES.

Ashleigh Brilliant

© ASHLEIGH BRILLIANT 1985. POT-SHOTS NO. 3988 Ashleigh Brilliant

AFTER I'VE MADE MYSELF PERFECT,

YOU'RE THE ONE I'M GOING TO WORK ON NEXT.

© ASHLEIGH BRILLIANT 1985. POT-SHOTS NO. 3722. Ashleigh Brilliant

THE BIGGEST ADVANTAGE OF NOT DOING THINGS VERY WELL

IS THAT IT OFTEN TAKES MUCH LESS TIME.

© ASHLEIGH BRILLIANT 1985. Ashleigh Brilliant POT-SHOTS NO. 3877.

THE ONLY REQUIREMENT FOR EVENTUALLY GETTING THERE

IS TO KEEP GOING IN THE RIGHT DIRECTION.

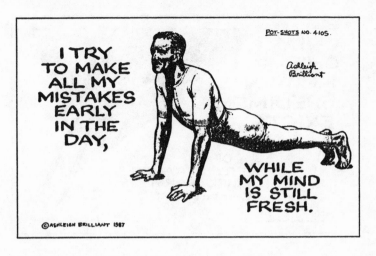

I TRY TO MAKE ALL MY MISTAKES EARLY IN THE DAY, WHILE MY MIND IS STILL FRESH.

POT-SHOTS NO. 4105.

©ASHLEIGH BRILLIANT 1987

April 17

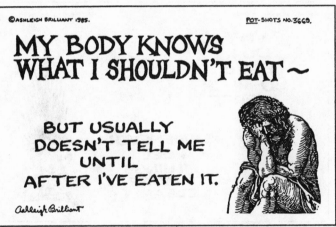

©ASHLEIGH BRILLIANT 1985.

POT-SHOTS NO. 3669.

MY BODY KNOWS WHAT I SHOULDN'T EAT ~

BUT USUALLY DOESN'T TELL ME UNTIL AFTER I'VE EATEN IT.

April 18

POT-SHOTS NO. 3705.

LOVE IS ALWAYS GOOD MEDICINE.

©ASHLEIGH BRILLIANT 1985.

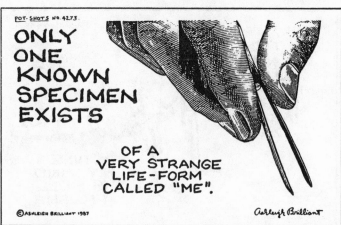

POT-SHOTS NO. 4273.

ONLY
ONE
KNOWN
SPECIMEN
EXISTS

OF A
VERY STRANGE
LIFE-FORM
CALLED "ME".

©ASHLEIGH BRILLIANT 1987

Ashleigh Brilliant

©ASHLEIGH BRILLIANT 1987.

POT-SHOTS NO. 4040.

WHY
DO I
FEEL
SO MUCH
WORSE

WHENEVER
I SEE
THINGS
MORE
CLEARLY?

Ashleigh Brilliant

©ASHLEIGH BRILLIANT 1985.

POT-SHOTS NO. 3954.

Ashleigh Brilliant

A GOOD WAY
TO BE AWARE
OF WHAT'S GOING ON
IS TO BECOME
A PART OF IT.

April 22

© ASHLEIGH BRILLIANT 1985.   POT-SHOTS NO. 3740

IF GOD
SERIOUSLY PLANS
TO HELP WITH
MY PROBLEMS,

HE HAS
A BUSY DAY
AHEAD OF HIM.

Ashleigh Brilliant

April 23

POT-SHOTS NO. 4114.

DON'T
EXPECT ME
TO BE
PERFECT
ALL THE
TIME,

BUT
PLEASE
RECOGNIZE
IT
WHEN
I AM.

© ASHLEIGH BRILLIANT 1987.

Ashleigh Brilliant

April 24

© ASHLEIGH BRILLIANT 1987.   POT-SHOTS NO. 4278.

REGARDLESS
OF WHAT
YOU'VE LOST,

WHAT MATTERS
IS
WHAT YOU DO
WITH
WHAT YOU HAVE LEFT.

Ashleigh Brilliant

POT-SHOTS NO. 3991.

WHAT RIGHT
DO YOU HAVE
TO
ENCOURAGE ME,

IF
I DON'T
WANT TO BE
ENCOURAGED?

Ashleigh
Brilliant
©ASHLEIGH BRILLIANT 1985.

©ASHLEIGH BRILLIANT 1985.   POT-SHOTS NO. 3688.

TRY IF YOU CAN
TO BELIEVE THAT,
EVEN WHEN
YOU'RE NOT
THINKING ABOUT ME,
I'M
STILL
HERE.

Ashleigh Brilliant

©ASHLEIGH BRILLIANT 1985.   POT-SHOTS NO. 3640.

I'M SHOOTING FORWARD
AT THE
TERRIFYING
SPEED

OF
60 MINUTES
PER
HOUR!

Ashleigh
Brilliant

© ASHLEIGH BRILLIANT 1985.

POT-SHOTS NO. 3883.

I HAVE MANY UNRECOGNIZED TALENTS ~

BUT MY FAULTS HAVE SOMEHOW SUCCEEDED IN SECURING WIDE RECOGNITION.

Ashleigh Brilliant

April 29

© ASHLEIGH BRILLIANT 1985.

POT-SHOTS NO. 3535.

Ashleigh Brilliant

ALL I WANT IS YOU BY MY SIDE,

AND WHATEVER ELSE YOU WILL LET ME HAVE.

© ASHLEIGH BRILLIANT 1987.

POT-SHOTS NO. 4065.

MY PROBLEM IS NOT CONTROLLING MY DESIRES ~

IT'S CONTROLLING YOURS.

Ashleigh Brilliant

Pot-Shots

BY ASHLEIGH BRILLIANT

POT-SHOTS NO. 4009.

For me,
it's always
easy to choose
between
the Ultimate,
the Infinite,
and
the Chocolate.

Ashleigh
Brilliant

III. May-Tricks

As far as its status as a month is concerned, there is nothing may-or-may-not about May. It is definitely here to stay, for 31 days, and will very likely have a big effect on what happens in June. The origin of its name, however, is somewhat less certain, and indeed may or may not derive from another member of that eclectic club, the Roman Pantheon—a goddess of agricultural growth and increase called Maia.

The arrival of May invariably produces strange urges to dance around suspiciously symbolic poles, or to parade through Red Square, honoring the Heroes of Labor. Later in the month, in a number of countries, a special day honors the heroes of another kind of labor, and goddesses of another kind of growth and increase, known as Mothers.

It is evidently a matrix-time, very suitable for giving form to great works. The mothers of Marx, Freud, Emerson, and Tchaikowsky all made their celebrated productions in May. For those already born, it is a good month, in Japan, to be a child (Children's Day, May 5), or, in Norway, to be a Norwegian (Constitution Day, May 13).

But, whatever your place or project, this is no month to hesitate. If, for some unaccountable reason, all you need, in order to go ahead, is my consent, take heart! Assuming that your intentions are honorable (and that I bear no responsibility for the outcome), my verdict is clear: Yes, You May!

© ASHLEIGH BRILLIANT 1985.

POT-SHOTS NO. 3541.

I WAS
UNEMPLOYED
FOR
A LONG
TIME,
BUT COULDN'T
ADJUST TO
THE HOURS.

Ashleigh Brilliant

© ASHLEIGH BRILLIANT 1985.

POT-SHOTS NO. 3838.

MY PROBLEMS AREN'T BIG

BUT IT DOESN'T
NECESSARILY
TAKE
A BIG PROBLEM
TO KILL ME.

© ASHLEIGH BRILLIANT 1985.

POT-SHOTS NO. 3693.

THE
ONLY
COMPLETELY
UNCENSORED
THINKING
I DO

IS CALLED
DREAMING.

Ashleigh Brilliant

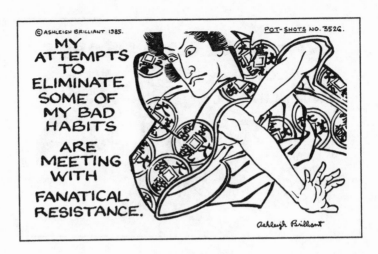

© ASHLEIGH BRILLIANT 1985. POT-SHOTS NO. 3526.

MY ATTEMPTS TO ELIMINATE SOME OF MY BAD HABITS ARE MEETING WITH FANATICAL RESISTANCE.

POT-SHOTS NO. 3569.

THERE ARE TIMES WHEN I HAVE TO BE HONEST WITH MYSELF, BUT, WITH LUCK, THEY SOON PASS.

© ASHLEIGH BRILLIANT 1985.

© ASHLEIGH BRILLIANT 1987. POT-SHOTS NO. 4248.

IF I CAN'T HAVE A GOOD FRIEND, AT LEAST LET ME FIND A WORTHY OPPONENT.

© ASHLEIGH BRILLIANT 1985. POT-SHOTS NO. 3840.

WHY ARE BAD PEOPLE USUALLY SO UNWILLING TO ADMIT HOW BAD THEY ARE?

Ashleigh Brilliant

© ASHLEIGH BRILLIANT 1987. POT-SHOTS NO. 4322.

MANY OTHERWISE NORMAL PEOPLE IN OUR SOCIETY SUFFER FROM A SEVERE HANDICAP CALLED PARENTHOOD.

Ashleigh Brilliant

© ASHLEIGH BRILLIANT 1987. POT-SHOTS NO. 4072.

THE EASIEST WAY TO BE THE BEST IS TO BE THE ONLY ONE OF YOUR KIND.

Ashleigh Brilliant

May 10

POT-SHOTS NO. 4205

One thing
I'm quite
capable
of doing
entirely
by myself
is:
getting
lost.

©ASHLEIGH BRILLIANT 1987.

May 11

©ASHLEIGH BRILLIANT 1987.   POT-SHOTS NO. 4017.

ONE INTERESTING THING
ABOUT MY LIFE STORY
    IS THAT I PLAY
        BOTH THE HERO
            AND THE VILLAIN.

May 12

©ASHLEIGH BRILLIANT 1987.   POT-SHOTS NO. 4150.

ALL MY
THOUGHTS
HAVE
ONE THING
IN COMMON:

THEY'RE ALL
MY THOUGHTS.

Ashleigh Brilliant

© ASHLEIGH BRILLIANT 1985.   POT- SHOTS NO. 3736.

IT'S
UNLUCKY
TO BE
SUPERSTITIOUS.

Ashleigh Brilliant

© ASHLEIGH BRILLIANT 1987.   POT- SHOTS NO. 4152.

IF YOU'RE
DETERMINED
TO BE
BRAVE
AND DARING,

YOU SHOULD
ALSO
TRY TO BE
VERY LUCKY.

Ashleigh Brilliant

© ASHLEIGH BRILLIANT 1985   POT- SHOTS NO. 3683.

IF YOU LOVED ME
FOR A SPLIT-SECOND,

IT
WOULD BE
THE MOST
WONDERFUL
SPLIT-SECOND
OF
MY LIFE.

Ashleigh Brilliant

May 16

© ASHLEIGH BRILLIANT 1985.

POT-SHOTS NO. 3858

ALL I REALLY NEED FOR MORE CONTROL OVER THE WORLD

IS MORE CONTROL OVER MYSELF.

Ashleigh Brilliant

May 17

© ASHLEIGH BRILLIANT 1987.

POT-SHOTS NO. 4090.

Ashleigh Brilliant

RELAX!

Your only purpose in this life

may be to rest and recover from some previous life.

May 18

© ASHLEIGH BRILLIANT 1985.

POT-SHOTS NO. 3725.

Ashleigh Brilliant

YOU CAN GET ANYWHERE FROM ANYWHERE:

DON'T WAIT TO BE SURE YOU'RE STARTING FROM THE RIGHT PLACE.

© ASHLEIGH BRILLIANT 1985.

POT-SHOTS NO. 3780.

Ashleigh Brilliant

I WISH I COULD ALWAYS ENJOY THE FAMILIAR

AS IF IT WERE VERY SPECIAL.

© ASHLEIGH BRILLIANT 1987.

POT-SHOTS NO. 4239.

Ashleigh Brilliant

IF YOU CAN'T FIND ANY OTHER MEANING IN EVERYTHING THAT'S HAPPENING,

TRY TO CONSIDER IT AS ENTERTAINMENT.

© ASHLEIGH BRILLIANT 1985.

POT-SHOTS NO. 3842.

Ashleigh Brilliant

BEING HUMAN MEANS I AM ENTITLED TO MAKE OCCASIONAL MISTAKES,

BUT AM ALSO ABLE TO REGRET THEM.

May 22

© ASHLEIGH BRILLIANT 1987.   POT-SHOTS NO. 4219.

IF
ONE OF US
THINKS
IT'S FUNNY
AND
ONE DOESN'T,

ONE OF US
MUST
BE
WRONG.

Ashleigh Brilliant

May 23

© ASHLEIGH BRILLIANT 1987.   POT-SHOTS NO. 4227.

DOES YOUR HEART
CONTAIN

ANYTHING
BREAKABLE?

Ashleigh Brilliant

May 24

© ASHLEIGH BRILLIANT 1985.   POT-SHOTS NO. 3654.

IF I COULD BE AT HOME
WHEREVER I GO,

WHAT
WOULD BE
THE POINT
OF GOING
ANYWHERE?

Ashleigh Brilliant

©ASHLEIGH BRILLIANT 1987. POT-SHOTS NO. 4028.

I like the World so much that I'm gradually letting it have its way with me.

©ASHLEIGH BRILLIANT 1985. POT-SHOTS NO. 3742

A HANDSOME REWARD IS OFFERED TO ANYBODY WHO CAN PROVE I'M WRONG,

BUT REFRAINS FROM DOING SO.

Ashleigh Brilliant

©ASHLEIGH BRILLIANT 1985. POT-SHOTS NO. 3577.

IT MAY BE WEEKS, OR EVEN MONTHS

BEFORE I DECIDE WHAT TO DO TOMORROW.

Ashleigh Brilliant

May 28

May 29

May 30

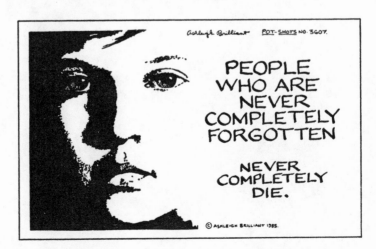

© ASHLEIGH BRILLIANT 1985.

POT-SHOTS NO. 3556.

YOU CAN
LEARN
MUCH
FROM HOW
PEOPLE MOVE
THEIR HANDS
AND BODIES,

SUCH AS,
WHERE
THEY ITCH.

Ashleigh Brilliant

IV. June and Tonic

June at last! Or, not June again! Depending on whether you live in the top or bottom half of the Earth (which in turn depends on which way is up), this month is in all likelihood going to bring you your longest or shortest period of continuous sunlight in that strange procession of celestial events which we call a year. Assuming, then, that you like long days, this month can either be a tonic to you, or put you in need of one.

An old tradition says that it is unlucky to get married on any day of the year whatsoever. But June has come to be particularly associated with that odd activity. I myself was once involved in such an incident (Temple Emanu-el, San Francisco, June 28, 1968). It is one of those experiences after which you are never quite the same, although the other party may come to consider you far too little changed (or, in some cases, too much).

According to some authorities, the name June derives from a Latin word meaning youth. Youth is another phenomenon which I have personally experienced. In my case, it was quite transitory, and seems to have ended sometime around June 28, 1968.

June also saw the assassination which precipitated the First World War (1914), two great invasions of the Second (1941 and 1944), and the signing of the United Nations Charter (1945), which might have prevented both wars, but came a little too late.

What will this June mean in your own life?—Thirty more opportunities, no doubt, to be baffled or bemused, tormented or tickled by the world—(whichever condition best meets your circumstances). Such symptoms do tend to be chronic, so I can only hope that the overall effect will be tonic.

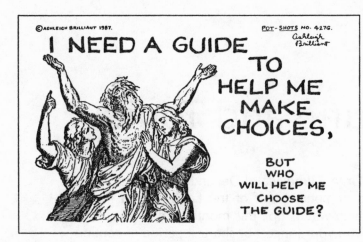

© ASHLEIGH BRILLIANT 1987.   POT-SHOTS NO. 4276.   Ashleigh Brilliant

I NEED A GUIDE TO HELP ME MAKE CHOICES, BUT WHO WILL HELP ME CHOOSE THE GUIDE?

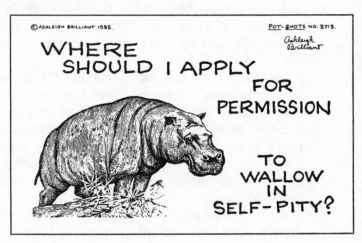

© ASHLEIGH BRILLIANT 1985.   POT-SHOTS NO. 3713.   Ashleigh Brilliant

WHERE SHOULD I APPLY FOR PERMISSION TO WALLOW IN SELF-PITY?

© ASHLEIGH BRILLIANT 1985.   POT-SHOTS NO. 3563.

WHY DOES NEARLY EVERYBODY NEARLY ALWAYS HAVE SOMETHING MORE IMPORTANT TO BE CONCERNED ABOUT THAN MY HAPPINESS?

Ashleigh Brilliant

June 4

© ASHLEIGH BRILLIANT 1985.   POT-SHOTS NO. 3670.

SOMETIMES I LOVE YOU
FOR WHAT
YOU ARE,

SOMETIMES
IN SPITE OF
WHAT YOU ARE.

Ashleigh Brilliant

June 5

© ASHLEIGH BRILLIANT 1987.   POT-SHOTS NO. 4291.

IT CAN TAKE
MUCH LONGER
THAN A LIFETIME
TO HAVE ANY
REAL SUCCESS
IN THIS WORLD.

Ashleigh Brilliant

June 6

© ASHLEIGH BRILLIANT 1985.   POT-SHOTS NO. 3663.

MAN THE
BATTLE STATIONS!

Ashleigh Brilliant

SOMEBODY'S
COMING
WHO WANTS
TO REASON
WITH US.

© ASHLEIGH BRILLIANT 1985.   POT-SHOTS NO. 3833.

I'M ALWAYS READY TO BE FRIENDS AGAIN —

AS SOON AS
THE DEEP WOUNDS
YOU'VE INFLICTED
HAVE HEALED.

Ashleigh Brilliant

© ASHLEIGH BRILLIANT 1985.   POT-SHOTS NO. 3612.

Ashleigh Brilliant

I seem to have
a special ability
to write
the kind of letters
which
never
bring
replies.

© ASHLEIGH BRILLIANT 1987.   POT-SHOTS NO. 4235.

THE MERE FACT
THAT
A RELATIONSHIP
HAS LASTED
A LONG TIME

DOESN'T
NECESSARILY
JUSTIFY

STRETCHING
IT FURTHER.

Ashleigh Brilliant

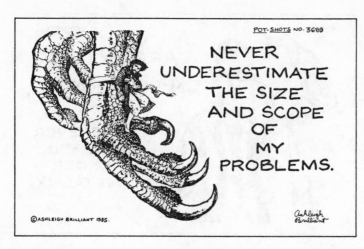

POT-SHOTS NO. 3689

NEVER
UNDERESTIMATE
THE SIZE
AND SCOPE
OF
MY
PROBLEMS.

©ASHLEIGH BRILLIANT 1985.

POT-SHOTS NO. 4032.

The best cure
for boredom
is
continual change ~

but even that
can become
boring.

©ASHLEIGH BRILLIANT 1987.

©ASHLEIGH BRILLIANT 1985.

POT-SHOTS NO. 3618.

I BELIEVE
THE STARS CAN
AFFECT HUMAN LIVES,

PARTICULARLY
BY
PROVIDING
EMPLOYMENT
FOR
THOUSANDS
OF
ASTROLOGERS.

June 16

POT-SHOTS NO. 3542.   Ashleigh Brilliant

YOU CAN'T STOP PROGRESS, BUT YOU CAN HELP DECIDE WHAT IS PROGRESS AND WHAT ISN'T.

© ASHLEIGH BRILLIANT 1985.

June 17

© ASHLEIGH BRILLIANT 1985.   POT-SHOTS NO. 3580.

DEFEAT IS NOT NECESSARILY FATAL ~ THAT'S WHY THE WORLD SEEMS TO BE SO FULL OF LOSERS.

Ashleigh Brilliant

June 18

© ASHLEIGH BRILLIANT 1985.   Ashleigh Brilliant   POT-SHOTS NO. 3679.

TO MOST PEOPLE I'M NOBODY ~ BUT WHAT MATTERS IS BEING SOMEBODY TO EVERYBODY WHO'S SOMEBODY TO ME.

© ASHLEIGH BRILLIANT 1985.

POT-SHOTS NO. 3864.

Ashleigh Brilliant

I STILL APPRECIATE YOU,

EVEN IF EVERYBODY ELSE DOES TOO.

© ASHLEIGH BRILLIANT 1985.

POT-SHOTS NO. 3793.

ONE VERY MYSTERIOUS THING ABOUT LIFE

IS THAT OCCASIONALLY SOME PIECE OF IT WILL SEEM PERFECTLY UNDERSTANDABLE.

Ashleigh Brilliant

© ASHLEIGH BRILLIANT 1987.

POT-SHOTS NO. 4063.

Whether I deserve it or not, I give myself another chance every day.

Ashleigh Brilliant

June 22

© ASHLEIGH BRILLIANT 1985.

POT-SHOTS NO. 3782.

Ashleigh Brilliant

MANY THINGS
NEED REASONS,

BUT
BEAUTIFUL THINGS
ARE ALLOWED
TO BE
BEAUTIFUL
FOR NO
REASON AT ALL.

June 23

© ASHLEIGH BRILLIANT 1987.

POT-SHOTS NO. 4269.

ANY GOD YOU FIND
WITHIN
YOURSELF

WOULD
PROBABLY
BE
VERY HARD
TO
LOSE AGAIN.

Ashleigh Brilliant

June 24

© ASHLEIGH BRILLIANT 1987.   Ashleigh Brilliant   POT-SHOTS NO. 4082.

How
does it
feel
to be
one of
several
billion
lords
of a
beautiful, mysterious planet?

POT-SHOTS NO. 3525.

WHY DO
SO MANY THINGS
THAT I DON'T
KNOW WHAT
TO DO ABOUT

CONSIDER
THEMSELVES
MY
RESPONSIBILITY?

©ASHLEIGH BRILLIANT 1985.

©ASHLEIGH BRILLIANT 1987.

POT-SHOTS NO. 4260.

THERE'S NOTHING WRONG
WITH
HAPPINESS,

SO LONG AS
YOU DON'T TRY
TO INFLICT YOURS
ON
OTHER PEOPLE.

Ashleigh Brilliant

©ASHLEIGH BRILLIANT 1987.

POT-SHOTS NO. 4077.

HAVING THE COURAGE
TO ADMIT DEFEAT

CAN
SOMETIMES BE

A KIND
OF

VICTORY.

©ASHLEIGH BRILLIANT 1985.
POT-SHOTS NO. 3892.

WHY
IS THERE
NO
MONUMENT
TO THE
UNKNOWN
HUSBAND?

Ashleigh Brilliant

©ASHLEIGH BRILLIANT 1985.
POT-SHOTS NO. 3750.

HOW I AM

DEPENDS ENTIRELY
ON
WHAT YOU MEAN
BY "HOW",
BY "I",
AND BY "AM".

Ashleigh Brilliant

©ASHLEIGH BRILLIANT 1987.
POT-SHOTS NO. 4250.

THERE'S NOTHING
YOU CAN DO
ABOUT
HOW OLD YOU ARE,

EXCEPT
CHANGE IT
BY GETTING
EVEN OLDER.

Ashleigh Brilliant

Pot-Shots BY **ASHLEIGH BRILLIANT**

POT-SHOTS NO. 4177.

NOT BEING ABLE TO DO EVERYTHING

IS NO
EXCUSE
FOR NOT DOING
EVERYTHING YOU CAN.

v. Jul-Eye-Pieces

The Romans were men of vision. (Although they loved spectacles, they did not wear them.) Julius Caesar, however, having very generously given his own name to this month early in 44 B.C., failed to foresee that he would be (rather spectacularly) assassinated in March of that same year. He himself therefore never had a chance to enjoy a single July. But we have been spending 31 days of every year since then paying tribute to his memory.

Perhaps in commemoration of its namesake's unfortunate end, July has become a popular month for revolutionary activities of all kinds. It is (apparently) a good time to break away from your mother country (U.S.A., July 4), storm your local Bastille (France, July 14), hail your Liberator (South America, Bolivar's Birthday, July 24), achieve your nationhood (Canada Day, July 1), or simply wipe out your current ruling family (Russia, July 17, 1918).

It was in July of 1969 that something even more revolutionary took place, about 400,000 kilometers from where I am writing, when two gentlemen claiming to represent the entire human species took up a short residence on the surface of the Moon. I myself had not been consulted about this, but was able to observe the event through the eye-piece of my living-room television set. "This", I thought, "means the end of the world as we know it." But I was wrong. Many July's have passed since then, and the world is still the world as we know it.

©ASHLEIGH BRILLIANT 1987.   POT-SHOTS NO. 4088.

WHY DO WE SUFFER
GREAT EVILS
IN SILENCE,

YET PROTEST
SO LOUDLY
AGAINST
MINOR
INCONVENIENCE?

Ashleigh Brilliant

©ASHLEIGH BRILLIANT 1987   POT-SHOTS NO. 4013.

FOR MAXIMUM SAFETY,
TRY NEVER TO BECOME
A SYMBOL
OF
ANYTHING
VERY
UNPOPULAR.

Ashleigh Brilliant

©ASHLEIGH BRILLIANT 1987.   POT-SHOTS NO. 4117.

SOMETIMES
I GET TIRED
OF BEING CREATIVE,

AND JUST
WANT TO DO
WHAT
EVERYBODY
ELSE
IS DOING.

Ashleigh Brilliant

July 4

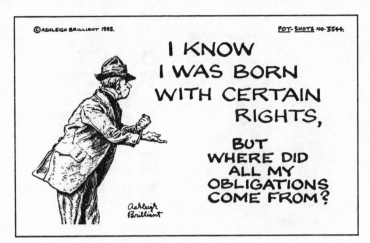

© ASHLEIGH BRILLIANT 1985.

POT-SHOTS NO. 3544.

I KNOW I WAS BORN WITH CERTAIN RIGHTS, BUT WHERE DID ALL MY OBLIGATIONS COME FROM?

Ashleigh Brilliant

July 5

© ASHLEIGH BRILLIANT 1985.

POT-SHOTS NO. 3770.

TODAY IS NOT YESTERDAY BUT SOMETIMES THEY'RE SO SIMILAR, IT'S HARD TO TELL THE DIFFERENCE.

Ashleigh Brilliant

July 6

POT-SHOTS NO. 3776. Ashleigh Brilliant

IT'S OBVIOUS THAT THE EARTH IS STILL CHANGING: WHAT'S NOT SO OBVIOUS IS ITS INTENDED FINAL FORM.

© ASHLEIGH BRILLIANT 1985.

© ASHLEIGH BRILLIANT 1985.   POT-SHOTS NO. 3674.

DON'T TRUST THE FUTURE ~

IT LOVES TO SPRING SURPRISES.

Ashleigh Brilliant

© ASHLEIGH BRILLIANT 1985.   POT-SHOTS NO. 3531.

IF YOU CAN'T GET RELIGION,

AT LEAST GET NUTRITION.

Ashleigh Brilliant

© ASHLEIGH BRILLIANT 1987.   POT-SHOTS NO. 4221.

Ashleigh Brilliant

FEELING BAD MAKES ME LOOK BAD —

But knowing that I look bad makes me feel worse.

July 10

© ASHLEIGH BRILLIANT 1985.   POT-SHOTS NO. 3948.

SLEEP IS SO WONDERFUL,

IT SHOULDN'T BE WASTED ON PEOPLE WHO ARE TOO TIRED TO ENJOY IT.

Ashleigh Brilliant

July 11

POT-SHOTS NO. 3851   *Ashleigh Brilliant*

I'm still not sure whether the end of my life will be a landing or a taking-off.

© ASHLEIGH BRILLIANT 1985.

July 12

© ASHLEIGH BRILLIANT 1987.   POT-SHOTS NO. 4023.

REALITY HAS SUCH A BIG FACE

THAT IT'S IMPOSSIBLE TO FACE ALL OF IT AT ONCE.

Ashleigh Brilliant

POT-SHOTS NO. 4096.

IS IT
ASKING
TOO MUCH
TO WANT
MY
LIFE STORY
TO HAVE
A HAPPY
ENDING?

©ASHLEIGH BRILLIANT 1987   *Ashleigh Brilliant*

©ASHLEIGH BRILLIANT 1985.   POT-SHOTS NO. 3560.

MY BIGGEST
PROBLEM
WITH MY
SKIN

IS
TRYING
TO
CONTROL
WHAT'S
INSIDE
IT.

Ashleigh Brilliant

©ASHLEIGH BRILLIANT 1985.   POT-SHOTS NO. 3594.

Ashleigh Brilliant

I NEED
TO FEEL
IMPORTANT:

ISN'T THERE
SOMEBODY
WHO HAS A NEED
TO MAKE ME
FEEL IMPORTANT?

© ASHLEIGH BRILLIANT 1987. POT-SHOTS NO. 4076.

SOMEWHERE
THE GHOSTS OF
THE PEOPLE
WE ONCE WERE

ARE
LAUGHING
AND CRYING
AT
WHAT
WE'VE
BECOME.

Ashleigh Brilliant

© ASHLEIGH BRILLIANT 1985. POT-SHOTS NO. 3846.

IT CAN SEEM
A LONG TIME
FROM BIRTH TO DEATH,

IF
YOU DON'T
HAVE
ENOUGH
TO DO.

Ashleigh Brilliant

© ASHLEIGH BRILLIANT 1987 POT-SHOTS NO. 4220.

I'M NOT REALLY DISORDERLY—

IT'S JUST THAT,
FOR MY KIND
OF ORDER,
THERE'S NEVER
ENOUGH
SPACE.

Ashleigh Brilliant

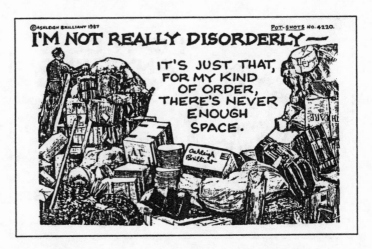

© ASHLEIGH BRILLIANT 1985. POT-SHOTS NO. 3559.

MANY SITUATIONS CAN BE EFFECTIVELY DEALT WITH

ONLY BY A VIGOROUS SHRUGGING OF THE SHOULDERS.

July 20

© ASHLEIGH BRILLIANT 1985. POT-SHOTS NO. 3735.

HOW CAN THE WORLD BE IMPROVING, WHEN WHAT WE ONCE CALLED "HEAVEN" WE NOW CALL "SPACE"?

July 21

© ASHLEIGH BRILLIANT 1987. POT-SHOTS NO. 4086.

I CAN DO ANYTHING I DECIDE TO DO ~

THE ONLY THING I CAN'T DO IS MAKE DECISIONS.

© ASHLEIGH BRILLIANT 1987.   POT-SHOTS NO. 4296.

IF I CAN'T REMEMBER ANYTHING ABOUT IT,

THE
CHANCES ARE,
I HAD
A VERY
GOOD TIME.

Ashleigh Brilliant

© ASHLEIGH BRILLIANT 1987.   POT-SHOTS NO. 4166.

NO MATTER
HOW IT TWISTS AND TURNS,

YOUR PAST
INEVITABLY LEADS TO
YOUR PRESENT.

Ashleigh Brilliant

POT-SHOTS NO. 3767.   © ASHLEIGH BRILLIANT 1985.

I'VE HAD
SOME OF
MY OPINIONS
FOR
SO LONG
THAT THEY
DON'T
FIT ME
ANY MORE.

Ashleigh Brilliant

©ASHLEIGH BRILLIANT 1987.

POT-SHOTS NO. 4315.

SLEEP WAS A MARVELLOUS INVENTION

BUT WHOEVER FIRST THOUGHT OF FILLING IT WITH **DREAMS** WAS TRULY INSPIRED.

Ashleigh Brilliant

POT-SHOTS NO. 3599.

PLEASE FORGIVE ME

FOR ALL THE NICE THINGS I NEVER SAID TO YOU.

©ASHLEIGH BRILLIANT 1985.

Ashleigh Brilliant

©ASHLEIGH BRILLIANT 1985.

POT-SHOTS NO. 3938.

THERE PROBABLY IS AN EASY ROAD TO SUCCESS~

THE TROUBLE IS, IT'S VERY HARD TO FIND.

Ashleigh Brilliant

©ASHLEIGH BRILLIANT 1985.   POT-SHOTS NO. 3857

DON'T INTERRUPT ME

WHILE I'M GIVING YOU MY UNDIVIDED ATTENTION.

Ashleigh Brilliant

©ASHLEIGH BRILLIANT 1987.   POT-SHOTS NO. 4145.

Ashleigh Brilliant

IT'S AMAZING HOW MANY OTHER THINGS PEOPLE WOULD RATHER DO

THAN

SPEND TIME WITH ME.

©ASHLEIGH BRILLIANT 1985.   *Ashleigh Brilliant*   POT-SHOTS NO. 3886.

WHETHER THE FUTURE LOOKS DARK OR BRIGHT

MAY IN EITHER CASE PROVE TO BE AN OPTICAL ILLUSION.

© ASHLEIGH BRILLIANT 1985.   POT-SHOTS No. 3901

THE SWEETEST
FORM OF
REVENGE
IS TO WIN
THE LOVE OF
YOUR ENEMY.

Ashleigh Brilliant

VI. Good Auguries

Not wishing to disappoint you if you were expecting this book, like some almanacs, to offer an assortment of insights into future events, I choose this point at which to prophesy, since it was the ancient prophetic practice of augury from which came "Augustus," the name of the first Roman Emperor, who in turn named this month after himself in what he probably never dreamed would one day be called the year 8 B.C.

Ancient augurers, believing that nothing happens by accident, looked for signs and portents in the entrails of sacrificial animals, and other strange places. I myself tend to be more concerned with activities in my own entrails, but I am also not so sure that accidents don't happen. In fact, I feel I can confidently predict that they will continue to do so. The trouble is, I can't tell you exactly when, where, and to whom, since this would obviously disqualify them as legitimate accidents.

My entrails do inform me, however, that there is not going to be any nuclear war (except by accident). And, if you are dissatisfied with the people currently in power, I can tell you that a whole new set of world leaders is coming along. Economic indicators will continue to fluctuate, but neither the good old days nor the bad old days will ever return. Science will keep failing to make us happy, while still enabling us to satisfy more and more of our deepest desires and fantasies. Best of all, I can assure you that, if you are alive today (please be very sure of this), the chances are excellent that you will find yourself alive tomorrow.

© ASHLEIGH BRILLIANT 1987.   POT-SHOTS NO. 4173.

LET THOSE WHO WANT WAR HAVE IT,

BUT ONLY IF THOSE WHO DON'T WANT IT AREN'T AFFECTED.

Ashleigh Brilliant

© ASHLEIGH BRILLIANT 1985.   Ashleigh Brilliant   POT-SHOTS NO. 3717

THE GREATEST TALENT OF ALL

IS BEING ABLE TO RECOGNIZE AND DEVELOP TALENT IN OTHER PEOPLE.

© ASHLEIGH BRILLIANT 1985.   POT-SHOTS NO. 3522.

IF YOU MUST KEEP GROANING,

PLEASE TRY TO DO IT IN A RHYTHM I CAN DANCE TO.

Ashleigh Brilliant

© ASHLEIGH BRILLIANT 1985. POT-SHOTS NO. 3704.

THERE'S NO GREATER SIN

THAN LETTING CHOCOLATE GET SO OLD THAT YOU HAVE TO THROW IT AWAY.

© ASHLEIGH BRILLIANT 1985. POT-SHOTS NO. 3746.

It's better to make friends with one small pussy-cat than to sit and curse the loneliness.

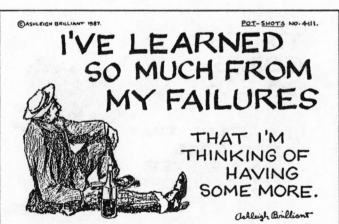

© ASHLEIGH BRILLIANT 1987. POT-SHOTS NO. 4111.

I'VE LEARNED SO MUCH FROM MY FAILURES

THAT I'M THINKING OF HAVING SOME MORE.

© ASHLEIGH BRILLIANT 1985.   POT-SHOTS NO. 3699.

WHY CAN'T I
BE CLOSER
TO THE PEOPLE
I NEVER MAKE
ANY EFFORT
TO GET
CLOSER TO?

Ashleigh Brilliant

© ASHLEIGH BRILLIANT 1987.   POT-SHOTS NO. 4217.

Ashleigh Brilliant

Whenever
I win
a struggle
against myself,
I always feel
great sympathy
for the loser.

© ASHLEIGH BRILLIANT 1985.   POT-SHOTS NO. 3650.

PERHAPS
MY TRUE
IDENTITY

IS THAT OF
A PERSON
WHO WILL
NEVER KNOW
MY
TRUE
IDENTITY.

Ashleigh Brilliant

© ASHLEIGH BRILLIANT 1987.   POT-SHOTS NO. 4048.

SOME PEOPLE WERE MEANT FOR EACH OTHER ~

OTHERS SHOULD AT ALL COSTS BE PREVENTED FROM EVER MEETING.

Ashleigh Brilliant

© ASHLEIGH BRILLIANT 1987.   POT-SHOTS NO. 4288

I'm glad not everybody wants to be immortal ~

IT LEAVES MORE ROOM FOR THE REST OF US.

Ashleigh Brilliant

© ASHLEIGH BRILLIANT 1987.   POT-SHOTS NO. 4300.

EXACTLY HOW FAR MUST I GO, AND IN WHICH DIRECTION,

TO GET AWAY FROM MYSELF?

Ashleigh Brilliant

August 16

© ASHLEIGH BRILLIANT 1987   POT-SHOTS NO. 4146.

MAYBE IT'S TIME FOR ANOTHER TRY

AT SOME OF THE THINGS YOU VOWED YOU'D NEVER ATTEMPT AGAIN.

Ashleigh Brilliant

© ASHLEIGH BRILLIANT 1987.   POT-SHOTS NO. 4281.

EVERYTHING IS UNDER CONTROL,

PERHAPS EVEN THE UNIVERSE.

Ashleigh Brilliant

August 17

August 18

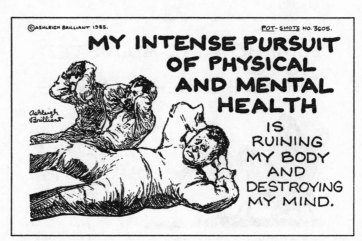

© ASHLEIGH BRILLIANT 1985.   POT-SHOTS NO. 3605.

MY INTENSE PURSUIT OF PHYSICAL AND MENTAL HEALTH

IS RUINING MY BODY AND DESTROYING MY MIND.

Ashleigh Brilliant

© ASHLEIGH BRILLIANT 1985. POT-SHOTS NO. 3951.

Isn't it surprising
how often
it does more good
to forget the past
than
to remember it.

Ashleigh Brilliant

© ASHLEIGH BRILLIANT 1987 POT-SHOTS NO. 4002

ASK YOURSELF THIS QUESTION:

WHY SHOULD I
LET ANYBODY
TELL ME
WHAT QUESTIONS
TO ASK MYSELF?

Ashleigh Brilliant

© ASHLEIGH BRILLIANT 1985. POT-SHOTS NO. 3794.

SOMEHOW I'VE ADJUSTED TO ALL LIFE'S OTHER CHANGES,

SO I SUPPOSE
I'LL ADJUST
TO
BECOMING
DEAD.

Ashleigh Brilliant

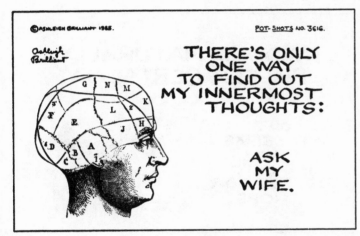

© ASHLEIGH BRILLIANT 1985.   POT-SHOTS NO. 3932.

WITH YOUR HELP,
I COULD PERFORM
A MIRACLE ~

THE
MIRACLE
WOULD
BE
TO
MAKE
YOU
LOVE ME.

Ashleigh Brilliant

August 26

© ASHLEIGH BRILLIANT 1985.   POT-SHOTS NO. 3810.

I WOULD NATURALLY
PREFER CERTAINTY,

BUT
IT SEEMS
I WILL
HAVE TO
SETTLE FOR
HOPE.

Ashleigh Brilliant

August 27

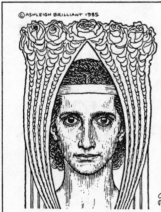

© ASHLEIGH BRILLIANT 1985.   POT-SHOTS NO. 3571.

AS
MY MIRROR
GETS OLDER,

IT GIVES
THE STRANGE
ILLUSION

OF ME·
GETTING
OLDER
TOO.

Ashleigh Brilliant

VII. Sep-Temper Tantrums

Anybody who has ever had SEPTuplets could tell you in a moment that SEPTember must originally have been the SEVENTH month of the year, not the ninth. The three months which follow it have had a similar undeserved fate, which, by the powers vested in me as author of this book, I am happy now at last to redress.

It has taken a long time. Incredible as it may seem, our whole civilization has persisted in this mockery for nigh on three thousand years. At any time since that day in 713 B.C. when the Romans, for reasons of their own, changed their minds and made January rather than March the first month of the year, somebody could have stood up and said, "Well, we now obviously have several months whose names are wrong, and something needs to be done about it." But nobody ever did—until now.

Seven (in Latin, Septem) is a number well-known for its magical and sacred qualities. We are told, on good authority, that the World was created in seven days. There are, or were supposed to be, Seven Seas, Seven Wonders of the World, Seven Deadly Sins, and (at least for Moslems) Seven Heavens. I feel this is a tradition worth hallowing, and will therefore now offer you my own contribution, which I hope you will find of equally mystical value—a list of SEVEN WONDER-FULS OF THE WORLD (according to Pot-Shots):

#3326: ISN'T IT WONDERFUL! INSIDE EVERY LITTLE BEAM OF LIGHT, A RAINBOW IS SLEEPING.

#2140: THERE'S A WONDERFUL METHOD OF RELIEVING FA-TIGUE CAUSED BY OVERWORK—IT'S CALLED "REST".

#1529: WORDS ARE A WONDERFUL FORM OF COMMUNICA-TION, BUT THEY WILL NEVER REPLACE KISSES AND PUNCHES.

#431: IF ONLY I COULD GET THAT WONDERFUL FEELING OF ACCOMPLISHMENT, WITHOUT HAVING TO ACCOMPLISH ANYTHING.

#3101: THE UNIVERSE SEEMS WONDERFUL IN THEORY, BUT IN PRACTICE I DON'T THINK IT WILL EVER WORK.

#3285: HOW WOULD YOU RATE ME, ON SCALE OF WONDER-FUL TO MARVELLOUS?

#2761: THE GREATEST WONDER IS HOW LITTLE TIME IT TAKES BEFORE ANY NEW WONDER NO LONGER SEEMS WONDER-FUL.

September 1

September 2

September 3

© ASHLEIGH BRILLIANT 1987.   POT-SHOTS NO. 4280.

HELP WANTED ~

PREVIOUS EXPERIENCE
IN TRYING TO HELP ME
NOT NECESSARY

(AND MAY
DISCOURAGE
YOU FROM
APPLYING).

© ASHLEIGH BRILLIANT 1985.   POT-SHOTS NO. 5855.

Can it be
that I have
the kind of
charm
best enjoyed
at a distance?

Ashleigh Brilliant

© ASHLEIGH BRILLIANT 1987.   POT-SHOTS NO. 4031.

MY DREAMS ARE SUBJECT
TO A VARIETY OF
INTERPRETATIONS ~

BUT
SO IS
MY
WAKING
LIFE.

Ashleigh Brilliant

POT-SHOTS NO. 3537. ©ASHLEIGH BRILLIANT 1985.

I BELIEVE IN GOOD HEALTH,

BUT NOT TO EXCESS.

Ashleigh Brilliant

©ASHLEIGH BRILLIANT 1985. POT-SHOTS NO. 3547.

WILL MAN EVER SUCCEED IN ESTABLISHING COMMUNICATION WITH WOMAN?

Ashleigh Brilliant

©ASHLEIGH BRILLIANT 1985. POT-SHOTS NO. 3609.

SOMETIMES I FEEL SAD FOR NO REASON AT ALL,

BUT THINKING ABOUT YOU GIVES ME PLENTY OF REASONS.

Ashleigh Brilliant

September 13

September 14

September 15

POT-SHOTS NO. 4246 ©ASHLEIGH BRILLIANT 1987.

I'D WANT TO GET TO KNOW YOU BETTER,

IF I WEREN'T SO AFRAID OF WHAT I MIGHT LEARN.

Ashleigh Brilliant

September 17

©ASHLEIGH BRILLIANT 1987.   POT-SHOTS NO. 4094.

WHEN WILL YOU BE FREE

TO BECOME MY CAPTIVE?

Ashleigh Brilliant

September 18

POT-SHOTS NO. 4127.

FOR BETTER OR WORSE, I'M EVENTUALLY GOING TO DIE,

SO I CAN ONLY HOPE IT'S FOR BETTER.

©ASHLEIGH BRILLIANT 1987.   *Ashleigh Brilliant*

September 19

September 20

September 21

© ASHLEIGH BRILLIANT 1985. POT-SHOTS NO. 3981.

HAVE YOU
NOTICED
HOW
EVERYBODY
IS
GETTING
OLDER?

Ashleigh Brilliant

© ASHLEIGH BRILLIANT 1987. POT-SHOTS NO. 4081.

LACK OF PUBLIC INTEREST
IN MY
PERSONAL
HAPPINESS
SEEMS TO BE
REACHING
EPIDEMIC
PROPORTIONS.

Ashleigh Brilliant

© ASHLEIGH BRILLIANT 1987. POT-SHOTS NO. 4266.

THERE WOULD HAVE TO BE
A BIG CHANGE IN YOU
TO SECURE
ANY CHANGE
WHATSOEVER
IN ME.

Ashleigh Brilliant

VIII. Caught in the Oct

Just how mistreated a month can be is clearly seen in the sorry case of October. Bad enough that for three millennia it has had to endure the indignity of tenth place in the calendar when it was originally eighth. (Octo = 8 in Latin). Even worse that in most of that time very little has ever happened, beyond an annual drinking orgy in Germany called the Oktoberfest, to cause its name to be widely acclaimed. Worst of all, just when something truly sensational finally did happen—the October Revolution of 1917 in Russia—the Soviets decided to change their calendar,—so that, although they still celebrate the anniversary of that great October Revolution, the celebration takes place in November!

St. Francis of Assisi, Miguel de Cervantes, Mahatma Gandhi, and Pablo Picasso were all born in October, although this was of interest, when it happened, only to their immediate families. It was also in October (1492) that Christopher Columbus stumbled upon something later called America, and that Martin Luther (in 1517) started something later called the Reformation. To any lover of Brilliant Thoughts, however, an even more important October anniversary is that of the world's first postcards, issued by the Austrian government in 1869. It took another 98 years before the ultimate purpose of this exciting new communication medium became apparent, with the publication of my own first Pot-Shots postcards, the official beginning of whatever it is that I have been doing ever since. The number 8 has until now lacked any particular distinction in our society, but I hope to fill this need by offering you the following list of EIGHT OUTSTANDING BRILLIANTS:[1]

[1] I am, among other things, the self-appointed world registrar of all people named BRILLIANT.

1. RICHARD BRILLIANT (b. 1929, Boston, Mass.). Scholar. Distinguished authority on Greek and Roman Art. Author of POMPEII A.D. 79: THE TREASURE OF REDISCOVERY.

2. LAWRENCE BRENT BRILLIANT (b. 1944, Detroit, Michigan). Physician and Epidemiologist. A leader in the totally successful campaign for worldwide eradication of smallpox.

3. FREDDA BRILLIANT (b. 1908, Lodz, Poland). Eminent sculptress. Her works include the Mahatma Gandhi Memorial, Tavistock Square, London.

4. DORA BRILLIANT. Russian Terrorist. Member of group called the Battle Organization. She made the bombs which killed Interior Minister Plehve (St. Petersburg, 1904) and Grand Duke Sergey (Moscow, 1905).

5. VARVARA ALEKSANDROVNA BRILLIANT (1888–1954). Soviet scientist, specializing in plant physiology. She discovered a method of stimulating photosynthesis known as the "Brilliant Phenomenon."

6. IRA FRANCIS BRILLIANT (b. 1922, New York City). Manuscript Collector and Philanthropist. Founder of the Ira F. Brilliant Center for Beethoven Studies at San Jose State University, California.

7. AMELIA BRILLIANT (b. Toronto, Canada). Distinguished and esteemed mother of No. 8.

8.   (Pardon my modesty).

October 1

October 2

October 3

October 4

© ASHLEIGH BRILLIANT 1987.

POT-SHOTS NO. 4184.

I'M GOING ON AN EATING-STRIKE,

AND WILL REFUSE TO STOP EATING UNTIL MY DEMANDS ARE MET.

Ashleigh Brilliant

DEMANDS

October 6

© ASHLEIGH BRILLIANT 1985.

POT-SHOTS NO. 3893.

ONCE I HAD ALL THE SECURITY ANYBODY COULD WANT ~

THEN, SUDDENLY, I WAS BORN.

Ashleigh Brilliant

October 7

© ASHLEIGH BRILLIANT 1987.

Ashleigh Brilliant

POT-SHOTS NO. 4277.

CAN THERE BE ANY GREATER TEST OF FAITH

THAN TO BELIEVE WHAT THE SCIENTISTS ARE TELLING US?

October 8

October 9

October 10

© ASHLEIGH BRILLIANT 1985.   POT-SHOTS NO. 3591.

IT'S NO USE
WORRYING,

BUT
ANY DAY
COULD BE
MY LAST.

POT-SHOTS NO. 3741

WHAT
I LIKE
MOST
ABOUT
ANIMALS

IS THAT
THEY ARE
SO
UNCIVILIZED.

© ASHLEIGH BRILLIANT 1986.

© ASHLEIGH BRILLIANT 1987.   POT-SHOTS NO. 4139.

IF YOU ONLY DO
WHAT'S IMPORTANT
YOU'LL NEVER HAVE
ANY FUN ~

UNLESS YOU CONSIDER
HAVING FUN IMPORTANT.

October 14

October 15

October 16

October 20

© ASHLEIGH BRILLIANT 1985.   POT-SHOTS NO. 3999.

DON'T JUDGE YOURSELF TOO HARSHLY —

LEAVE THAT TO ME.

Ashleigh Brilliant

October 21

© ASHLEIGH BRILLIANT 1985   Ashleigh Brilliant   POT-SHOTS NO. 3849.

Eleven years from now, the next ten years will be only a memory.

October 22

© ASHLEIGH BRILLIANT 1987.   POT-SHOTS NO. 4187.

GONE, BUT NOT FORGOTTEN:

THE CONFIDENCE I ONCE HAD IN MYSELF.

Ashleigh Brilliant

October 26

POT-SHOTS NO.4212.
THE BIGGER THE CHANCE OF LOSING, THE MORE EXCITEMENT THERE IS IN WINNING.
©ASHLEIGH BRILLIANT 1987.

October 27

©ASHLEIGH BRILLIANT 1985.
POT-SHOTS NO.3600.
I AM AN ORDERLY PERSON WHO JUST HAPPENS TO BE LIVING A DISORDERLY LIFE.
Ashleigh Brilliant

October 28

©ASHLEIGH BRILLIANT 1987.
POT-SHOTS NO.4213.
WHAT'S BUILT IN THE SAND SOON GETS WASHED AWAY: THAT'S WHY MAKING IT BEAUTIFUL IS SO IMPORTANT.

© ASHLEIGH BRILLIANT 1985. POT-SHOTS NO. 3552.

Ashleigh Brilliant

THE BASIC FACTS OF EXISTENCE ARE SO INCREDIBLE

THAT NO TRULY SANE PERSON COULD POSSIBLY BELIEVE THEM.

© ASHLEIGH BRILLIANT 1985. POT-SHOTS NO. 3538.

ANY CHANGE IN YOUR POSITION

WOULD BE WELCOME AS A SIGN OF LIFE.

Ashleigh Brilliant

© ASHLEIGH BRILLIANT 1987. POT-SHOTS NO. 4058.

Ashleigh Brilliant

DON'T IGNORE YOUR CHILD'S BIZARRE BEHAVIOR —

IT COULD BE SYMPTOMATIC OF A DISORDER CALLED GROWING UP.

ix. Novembursts

Except for any November in which you may happen to begin or end your life, this month, like April, June and September, always comes with a guaranteed (although slightly under par) supply of 30 days. Among those who had a short last November (in 397 A.D.) was Martin, the patron saint of France. November 11 became his feast day, and, in 1918, turned out to be the day on which the fighting stopped in one of France's (and the World's) worst wars.

For many Christians, November also brings All Saints Day, followed by All Souls Day. For Albanians, it brings Independence Day, followed by Liberation Day. For Americans, it brings Thanksgiving Day, followed (very often) by indigestion.

It is, of course, another in this foursome of mis-named months, running ninth in a race in which it is forever doomed to finish eleventh. And Nine (Novem in Latin) is another of those mysterious numbers with supposedly special powers. We invoke Nine Stitches Saved (by one taken in time), Nine Days' Wonders, and Nine Points of the Law. Cats are said to have Nine Lives (although humans have to gestate for Nine Months just to get one).

In keeping with these nifty nines, I have decided to present you with a very special Appendix, listing an extraordinary NINE OF MINE, consisting of nine of my licensed products which, for various reasons, are no longer being manufactured, and are therefore now eagerly sought by collectors (at least in my fantasies). You may not consider this very mystical, but please don't call it asiNINE. [See CALLING ALL COLLECTORS, p. 165].

POT-SHOTS NO. 3817. *Ashleigh Brilliant* ©ASHLEIGH BRILLIANT 1985.

THE GOVERNMENT CONTROLS THE PEOPLE

BY MAKING THE PEOPLE THINK THEY CONTROL THE GOVERNMENT.

©ASHLEIGH BRILLIANT 1987. POT-SHOTS NO. 4177.

NOT BEING ABLE TO DO EVERYTHING

IS NO EXCUSE FOR NOT DOING EVERYTHING YOU CAN.

Ashleigh Brilliant

©ASHLEIGH BRILLIANT 1987. POT-SHOTS NO. 4157.

The only difference between then and now

IS SOMETHING CALLED TIME.

Ashleigh Brilliant

© ASHLEIGH BRILLIANT 1987.

POT-SHOTS NO. 4249.

TIME IS SO PRECIOUS

YOU SHOULD ALWAYS BE DOING SOMETHING IMPORTANT,

OR PLEASANT,

(OR PREFERABLY BOTH).

Ashleigh Brilliant

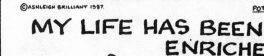

© ASHLEIGH BRILLIANT 1987.

POT-SHOTS NO. 4234.

MY LIFE HAS BEEN ENRICHED WITH MANY WONDERFUL INSIGHTS,

WHICH I HAVE NOW ENTIRELY FORGOTTEN.

Ashleigh Brilliant

© ASHLEIGH BRILLIANT 1985.

POT-SHOTS NO. 3764.

PERHAPS THE MAIN PURPOSE OF BEING AWAKE

IS TO HAVE SOMETHING TO DREAM ABOUT WHEN I'M ASLEEP.

Ashleigh Brilliant

November 10

November 11

November 12

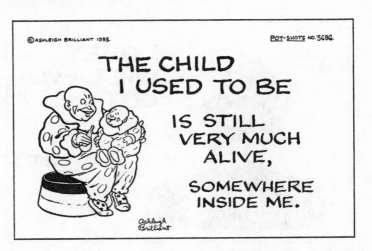

© ASHLEIGH BRILLIANT 1987.   POT-SHOTS NO. 4203.

WHAT MAKES
MY LOAD
SO
HEAVY
IS THAT
I HAVEN'T TIME
TO DECIDE
WHAT I DON'T NEED.

© ASHLEIGH BRILLIANT 1987.   POT-SHOTS NO. 4170.

IT'S PLEASANT
TO LOOK BACK ON
SOME THINGS
WHICH
I DIDN'T
ENJOY
LOOKING
FORWARD
TO.

Ashleigh Brilliant

© ASHLEIGH BRILLIANT 1985.   POT-SHOTS NO. 3911.

I OBEY
SOME LAWS
OUT OF
FEAR,

BUT MOST
JUST
OUT OF
HABIT.

November 16

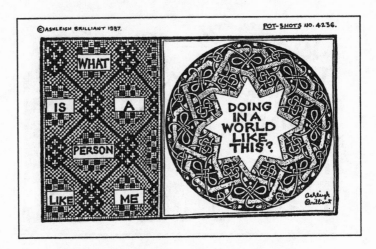

November 17

November 18

November 22

© ASHLEIGH BRILLIANT 1987.   Ashleigh Brilliant   POT- SHOTS NO. 4137.

I CAN'T
GO ON
LIKE
THIS

BUT
UNTIL
CIRCUMSTANCES
CHANGE,
I PROBABLY
WILL.

November 23

POT-SHOTS NO. 3931   © ASHLEIGH BRILLIANT 1985.

TODAY'S
NEWS
MUST HAVE
A MESSAGE
SOMEWHERE~

WHAT EXACTLY
IS IT TRYING
TO TELL US?

Ashleigh Brilliant

November 24

© ASHLEIGH BRILLIANT 1985.   POT- SHOTS NO. 3983.

I DON'T KNOW WHAT
I'M GOING TO DIE OF ~
BUT FOR PREFERENCE I'D CHOOSE
EXTREME SATISFACTION.

Ashleigh Brilliant

© ASHLEIGH BRILLIANT 1985.　　POT-SHOTS NO. 3986.

STOP
WORRYING!

EVERYTHING
WILL BE
THE SAME
AFTER
THE END
AS IT WAS
BEFORE
THE
BEGINNING.

© ASHLEIGH BRILLIANT 1985.　　POT-SHOTS NO. 3962.

IF WE COULD ALL HEAR
EACH OTHER'S
PRAYERS,

GOD
MIGHT BE
RELIEVED
OF SOME
OF HIS
BURDEN.

Ashleigh Brilliant

© ASHLEIGH BRILLIANT 1987.　　POT-SHOTS NO. 4138.

Ashleigh Brilliant

BY TAKING
MY
PROBLEMS
ONE AT
A TIME,

I CAN
MAKE
THEM
LAST
MUCH
LONGER.

November 28

© ASHLEIGH BRILLIANT 1985. POT-SHOTS NO. 3921.

FOLLOW YOUR INSTINCTS,

AND SEE HOW QUICKLY YOU GET INTO TROUBLE.

Ashleigh Brilliant

November 29

© ASHLEIGH BRILLIANT 1985. POT-SHOTS NO. 3651.

I was hoping that, by the time I got this far, I would have gotten much farther.

Ashleigh Brilliant

November 30

© ASHLEIGH BRILLIANT 1985. POT-SHOTS NO. 3899. *Ashleigh Brilliant*

IN A WORLD WITHOUT WAR,

THE MOST POWERFUL COUNTRIES WILL BE THOSE WITH THE BEST NEGOTIATORS.

x. Decem-Antics

You need only think of "decade" and "decimal" to see that December, like his three abused brothers, is two steps out of place. But if you wish to consider this the end of the year, or even of the book, those of us who are going on ask only that you leave quietly, without creating a disturbance.

If you were born in December, you are in the company of Beethoven, Milton, and Pasteur. If that is not sufficiently thrilling, you are also a month-mate of Yours Truly and his wife Dorothy (December 9 and 8). Isaac Newton was born on the 25th, which, had the date not been pre-empted, might by now be a big holiday known as Newtonmas, perhaps with apple-trees being set up indoors, and decorated for the occasion.

It is time again, around the 21st, for your shortest or longest day of the year, whichever of the two you didn't have last time in June (unless you sneaked across the Equator when I wasn't looking).

You can celebrate many things in December, but one that you can't—at least not officially—is the feast day of Saint Barbara, the patron saint of mariners, on December 4. It has been discontinued by the Catholic Church after some eighteen centuries of observance, because of (rather belated) doubts as to whether the lady in question ever really existed. This comes despite the fact that her name was permanently bestowed by Spanish explorers (in 1602) upon that part of the California coast in which (unknown to them) the very book you are now reading would some time later be written and published. I hope this unfortunate Saint, having been dropped from the Church's calendar, may take some small consolation at being remembered in mine.

The number Ten (Decem in Latin) is famous for its association with a certain set of Commandments—which makes this a very good place to give you my own TEN POT-SHOTS COM-MANDMENTS:

#209. DO WHAT YOU KNOW IS RIGHT, BUT TRY NOT TO GET CAUGHT.

#171. FORCE YOURSELF TO RELAX.

#91. USE YOUR OWN JUDGMENT—THEN DO AS I SAY.

#2022. CLING TO YOUR INSECURITY—IN THIS WORLD, IT'S THE ONLY THING YOU CAN BE SURE OF.

#2849. NEVER RESIST A MAD IMPULSE TO DO SOMETHING NICE FOR ME.

#2287. DON'T LET THEM DO TO US WHAT WE WOULD DO TO THEM IF THEY LET US.

#892. DON'T BE AFRAID TO GIVE SOME OF YOURSELF AWAY—IT WILL ALL GROW BACK.

#2452. TAKE CARE OF WHAT YOU LOVE, AND TRY TO LOVE WHATEVER YOU HAVE TO TAKE CARE OF.

#636. DON'T GIVE UP HOPE—UNLESS THE SITUATION IS OB-VIOUSLY HOPELESS.

#142. WHEN ALL ELSE FAILS, EAT!

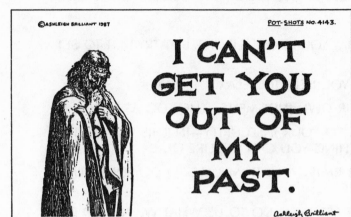

© ASHLEIGH BRILLIANT 1987 POT-SHOTS NO. 4143.

I CAN'T GET YOU OUT OF MY PAST.

Ashleigh Brilliant

© ASHLEIGH BRILLIANT 1985. POT-SHOTS NO. 3697

TUGGING IN OPPOSITE DIRECTIONS
IS AT LEAST ONE WAY OF STAYING TOGETHER.

Ashleigh Brilliant

© ASHLEIGH BRILLIANT 1985 POT-SHOTS NO. 3950.

I'VE DECIDED TO LIVE FOREVER,
BUT RESERVE THE RIGHT TO CHANGE MY MIND.

Ashleigh Brilliant

December 4

© ASHLEIGH BRILLIANT 1987.

POT-SHOTS NO. 4045

IT'S GOOD TO HAVE SOME CERTAINTY IN LIFE ~

EVEN IF IT'S ONLY THAT I'M IN DEEP TROUBLE.

Ashleigh Brilliant

© ASHLEIGH BRILLIANT 1985.

POT-SHOTS NO. 3757.

I SEEM TO BRING OUT THE MOTHER IN EVERYBODY,

EXCEPT MY MOTHER.

Ashleigh Brilliant

December 5

December 6

© ASHLEIGH BRILLIANT 1985.

POT-SHOTS NO. 3539.

I WOULD HAVE LIKED TO BE A VERY IMPORTANT PERSON,

BUT NOBODY EVER OFFERED ME THE ROLE.

Ashleigh Brilliant

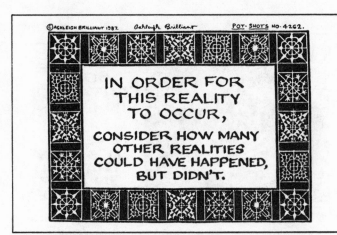

©ASHLEIGH BRILLIANT 1987. Ashleigh Brilliant POT-SHOTS NO. 4262.

IN ORDER FOR
THIS REALITY
TO OCCUR,
CONSIDER HOW MANY
OTHER REALITIES
COULD HAVE HAPPENED,
BUT DIDN'T.

©ASHLEIGH BRILLIANT 1985. POT-SHOTS NO. 3769.

LOVING ME
IS ALWAYS
WORTH
THE EFFORT.

Ashleigh Brilliant

Ashleigh Brilliant ©ASHLEIGH BRILLIANT 1985. POT-SHOTS NO. 3972.

I HOPE
YOUR
BIRTHDAY
IS A
SUCCESS,
AND BRINGS
MANY
ENCORE
PERFORMANCES.

December 10

© ASHLEIGH BRILLIANT 1987.   POT-SHOTS NO. 4142.

EVEN IN THE
FORESEEABLE
FUTURE,

THERE ARE
MANY THINGS
WHICH NOBODY
WILL HAVE
FORESEEN.

Ashleigh Brilliant

December 11

© ASHLEIGH BRILLIANT 1985.   POT-SHOTS NO. 3945.

THE OLDER YOU GET,

THE MORE
IMPORTANT
IT IS
NOT TO
ACT YOUR AGE.

Ashleigh Brilliant

December 12

© ASHLEIGH BRILLIANT 1985.   POT-SHOTS NO. 3523.
Ashleigh Brilliant

ALL I WANT IS
MORE AND MORE
AND MORE...

IS THAT
ASKING
TOO
MUCH?

© ASHLEIGH BRILLIANT 1985.   POT-SHOTS NO. 3978.

YOU ALWAYS
LOOK
YOUR BEST
AFTER
I'VE BEEN
WELL-FED.

Ashleigh Brilliant

December 14

© ASHLEIGH BRILLIANT 1987.   POT-SHOTS NO. 4169.

I'VE LOST
SOMETHING VALUABLE:

CONTACT
WITH
YOU.

Ashleigh Brilliant

© ASHLEIGH BRILLIANT 1987   POT-SHOTS NO. 4016.

IF YOU WAIT
PATIENTLY
ENOUGH,

EVENTUALLY
YOU WILL
REACH
THE END OF
YOUR
PATIENCE.

Ashleigh Brilliant

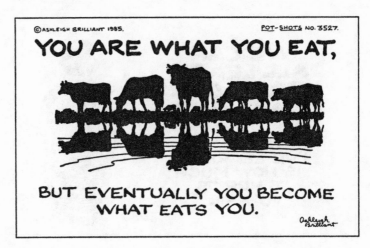

© ASHLEIGH BRILLIANT 1985

POT-SHOTS NO. 3959.

WE CAN ALL LEARN FROM OUR FAILURES

WHAT I'VE LEARNED IS HOW MUCH IT HURTS TO FAIL.

Ashleigh Brilliant

© ASHLEIGH BRILLIANT 1985.

POT-SHOTS NO. 3859.

IF NOTHING REALLY EXISTS BUT THE PRESENT MOMENT,

WHY DO SOME PAST MOMENTS STILL SEEM SO REAL?

Ashleigh Brilliant

© ASHLEIGH BRILLIANT 1985.

Ashleigh Brilliant

POT-SHOTS NO. 3684.

A GOOD NIGHT'S SLEEP

IS WORTH ITS WEIGHT IN DREAMS.

December 22

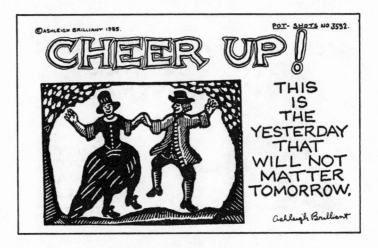

©ASHLEIGH BRILLIANT 1985.   POT-SHOTS NO. 3532.

CHEER UP!

THIS IS THE YESTERDAY THAT WILL NOT MATTER TOMORROW.

Ashleigh Brilliant

December 23

©ASHLEIGH BRILLIANT 1985.   POT-SHOTS NO. 3660.
Ashleigh Brilliant

OCCASIONALLY TWO SNOWFLAKES ARE FOUND TO BE IDENTICAL,

BUT THE NEWS IS IMMEDIATELY SUPPRESSED.

December 24

©ASHLEIGH BRILLIANT 1987.   POT-SHOTS NO. 4085.

My best reason for believing in God is my need for companionship.

Ashleigh Brilliant

© ASHLEIGH BRILLIANT 1987.
POT- SHOTS NO. 4121.

IT'S A WHOLE YEAR BETWEEN CHRISTMASES,

BUT IT'S ONLY A SHORT CHRISTMAS BETWEEN YEARS.

© ASHLEIGH BRILLIANT 1985.
POT- SHOTS NO. 3730.

What I need are problems that I can eat my way out of.

© ASHLEIGH BRILLIANT 1987.
POT- SHOTS NO. 4132.

If I can't have contentment, at least let me have an interesting variety of discontents.

134

December 28

December 29

December 30

XI. Janu-Worries

Many people seem to feel that a year, like anything else, has to get started somehow, and that January is here for that sole purpose. Other uses have, however, occasionally been found for it—as a dump for discarded holiday decorations, or as a convenient staging-ground for major and minor psychological depressions. The Romans apparently had all this in mind when they named it after Janus, a disturbingly schizoid god, with two faces, looking in opposite directions (presumably into the past and future), whom they placed symbolically in open doorways and associated with the idea of new beginnings.

Modern research has, however, proven that moving forward in time (if that is what we are doing), can, at least in some cases, be therapeutic. And the sense of being unready for whatever is to come, which many of us experience, must not be confused with actual fear and panic, which the rest of us are trying desperately to suppress.

One way of easing the strain is by resolving to make improvements during the coming year. One of my own perennial resolutions, as yet unfulfilled, is to start a movement aimed at softening the absurdly abrupt transition which currently finds us stepping out of December directly into a different, totally unfamiliar, year. The entire program is not yet clear in my mind, but we could certainly start by toning down that worrisome symbol of an unknown future waiting to swallow us up—the gaping, wide-open door. If we retain the door at all, it should be only slightly AJAR, and should indeed be so labelled, those being also the initials of my proposed organization's name and slogan: "All Januaries Are Ridiculous."

© ASHLEIGH BRILLIANT 1985.   POT-SHOTS NO. 3708.

Nobody
can say
that
I don't know
my own
two
minds.

Ashleigh Brilliant

POT-SHOTS NO. 3895.

I CAN
FACE
THE MONTHS
AND YEARS

WHAT TROUBLE ME
ARE THE HOURS
AND MINUTES.

Ashleigh Brilliant

© ASHLEIGH BRILLIANT 1985.

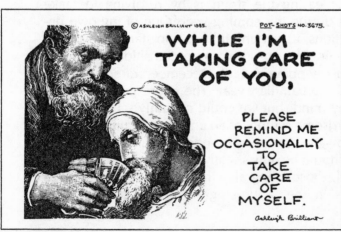

© ASHLEIGH BRILLIANT 1985.   POT-SHOTS NO. 3675.

WHILE I'M
TAKING CARE
OF YOU,

PLEASE
REMIND ME
OCCASIONALLY
TO
TAKE
CARE
OF
MYSELF.

Ashleigh Brilliant

© ASHLEIGH BRILLIANT 1987.
POT-SHOTS NO. 4223.

THERE I GO AGAIN ~

GETTING OLDER.

Ashleigh Brilliant

© ASHLEIGH BRILLIANT 1987.
POT-SHOTS NO. 4286.

YOU'D BE SURPRISED HOW OFTEN I HAD TO GO BACK

IN ORDER TO COME THIS FAR FORWARD

Ashleigh Brilliant

© ASHLEIGH BRILLIANT 1987.
Ashleigh Brilliant
POT-SHOTS NO. 4091.

I ONLY STAY AWAKE

TO HELP PASS THE TIME BETWEEN DREAMS.

January 10

POT-SHOTS NO. 3775. *Ashleigh Brilliant*

DON'T DESPAIR ~ HELP MAY BE COMING FROM AN UNEXPECTED SOURCE—

SOMEWHERE WITHIN YOU.

© ASHLEIGH BRILLIANT 1985.

January 11

THE MORE I WRESTLE WITH MY CONSCIENCE,

POT-SHOTS NO. 3712.

THE MORE WAYS I LEARN TO DEFEAT IT.

Ashleigh Brilliant

© ASHLEIGH BRILLIANT 1985.

January 12

© ASHLEIGH BRILLIANT 1985.

POT-SHOTS NO. 3862.
Ashleigh Brilliant

BEING ME IS A RISK WHICH I SOMETIMES WISH I'D NEVER TAKEN.

January 13

POT-SHOTS NO. 3758.

SOME BOOKS
MAKE ME
WANT TO
GO
ADVENTURING~

OTHERS
MAKE ME FEEL
THEY'VE
SAVED ME
THE TROUBLE.

© ASHLEIGH BRILLIANT 1985.

January 14

© ASHLEIGH BRILLIANT 1987.

POT-SHOTS NO. 4156.

FOREVER

DOESN'T ALWAYS
LAST
AS LONG AS
YOU THINK
IT WILL.

January 15

© ASHLEIGH BRILLIANT 1985.

POT-SHOTS NO. 3980.

BEFORE YOU BREAK
THE
RULES,

REMEMBER
THAT
SOCIETY
TOOK
A LONG
TIME
MAKING
THEM.

January 16

POT-SHOTS NO. 3958.   ©ASHLEIGH BRILLIANT 1985

WHY IS IT THAT I'M MOST AWARE OF MY BODY ONLY WHEN IT'S NOT WORKING PROPERLY?

January 17

©ASHLEIGH BRILLIANT 1987.   POT-SHOTS NO. 4042.

DON'T WORRY ABOUT KEEPING IN TOUCH WITH THE INEVITABLE ~

IT WILL ALWAYS KNOW WHERE TO FIND YOU.

January 18

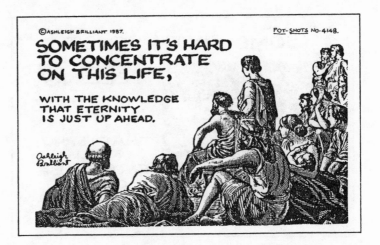

©ASHLEIGH BRILLIANT 1987.   POT-SHOTS NO. 4148.

SOMETIMES IT'S HARD TO CONCENTRATE ON THIS LIFE,

WITH THE KNOWLEDGE THAT ETERNITY IS JUST UP AHEAD.

©ASHLEIGH BRILLIANT 1985.   POT-SHOTS NO. 3583.

I AM ALWAYS
EXACT
AND
PRECISE

(MORE
OR
LESS).

Ashleigh
Brilliant

POT-SHOTS NO. 4190.
Ashleigh
Brilliant

The more
I need help,

the more
embarrassing
it is
to have to
ask for it.

©ASHLEIGH BRILLIANT 1987

©ASHLEIGH BRILLIANT 1985.   POT-SHOTS NO. 3557.

SOME SIXTH SENSE
KEEPS
TELLING
ME

THAT I'M NOT
MAKING
ENOUGH USE
OF THE
OTHER FIVE.

Ashleigh Brilliant

© ASHLEIGH BRILLIANT 1987.   POT-SHOTS NO. 4070.

YOU CAN HAVE AN EX-HUSBAND OR EX-WIFE

BUT YOU CAN'T HAVE AN EX-CHILD.

Ashleigh Brilliant

POT-SHOTS NO. 3977.

I HAVE GREAT SYMPATHY FOR THE UNDERDOG, ESPECIALLY WHEN THE UNDERDOG IS ME.

Ashleigh Brilliant

© ASHLEIGH BRILLIANT 1985.

© ASHLEIGH BRILLIANT 1985.   POT-SHOTS NO. 3881.

Ashleigh Brilliant

I'M FINDING IT HARD TO FUNCTION TODAY,

AFTER SPENDING ALL NIGHT IN A STRANGE TRANCE CALLED "SLEEP."

© ASHLEIGH BRILLIANT 1987.   POT-SHOTS NO. 4311.

THE BEST TIME TO LOOK FOR HELP IS BEFORE YOU NEED IT.

Ashleigh Brilliant

© ASHLEIGH BRILLIANT 1985.   POT-SHOTS NO. 3528.

MY MIND IS SO FULL OF IN-COMING MESSAGES, THERE'S VERY LITTLE ROOM FOR MY OWN THOUGHTS.

Ashleigh Brilliant

© ASHLEIGH BRILLIANT 1987.   POT-SHOTS NO. 4057.

Ashleigh Brilliant

DON'T EVER DO THAT AGAIN! FOR FURTHER DETAILS, CONSULT YOUR CONSCIENCE.

January 28

January 29

January 30

Ashleigh Brilliant

POT-SHOTS NO. 3550.

I HAVE DEFINITELY CHOSEN LIFE ~

BUT ONLY BECAUSE MY CHOICES WERE VERY LIMITED.

©ASHLEIGH BRILLIANT 1985.

XII. Feb-Ruminations

The 14th of this month, called St. Valentine's Day, has, for obscure reasons, become in many countries a day sacred to lovers, and (for reasons less obscure) to the sellers of greeting-cards. Love, of course, does not need special days, but card companies will probably continue to need them, at least until they succeed in their efforts to get a law passed declaring that every day is everybody's birthday.

Named for a yearly Roman ritual of repentance called the Februa, poor February atones for her own unknown sins with a lifespan both abbreviated and irregular. For this reason, you will find 29 days allotted herein, but, depending on just what particular February this happens to be, the last day should or should not be counted.

How to resolve this terrible uncertainty? There are only two ways I know of, apart from mathematical calculation or consulting some other source. Ask yourself (1) Are the Olympic Games being held this year? (2) Is there going to be an American presidential election this year?—If the answers are yes, then this is a Leap Year (probably so called from the association with Olympic leaping), and February will have an extra day (no doubt simply to stretch out the interminable election campaign one day longer). In all other years, this month will have only 28 days (which is at least a nice even number of weeks), and you will have to step carefully around February 29 on your way into March.

©ASHLEIGH BRILLIANT 1987.   Ashleigh Brilliant   POT-SHOTS NO. 4214.

NATURE IS NOT DIRTY ~
BUT NATURE SUPPLIES ALL THE RAW MATERIALS FROM WHICH WE MANUFACTURE DIRT.

POT-SHOTS NO. 4022. ©ASHLEIGH BRILLIANT 1987.

Today will be gone in an instant, but the past will be with us forever.
Ashleigh Brilliant

©ASHLEIGH BRILLIANT 1987.   POT-SHOTS NO. 4320.   Ashleigh Brilliant

I COULD ACCEPT DEATH MORE EASILY, IF I COULD BE SURE IT ONLY HAPPENS TO OTHER PEOPLE.

POT-SHOTS NO. 3843.

I FEEL
I SHOULD BE
A BETTER
FRIEND
TO YOU

THAN I
PROBABLY
EVER
WILL
BE.

©ASHLEIGH BRILLIANT 1985.

©ASHLEIGH BRILLIANT 1985.

POT-SHOTS NO. 3653.

SAVE
TIME —
LIVE
SEVERAL LIVES
AT ONCE.

©ASHLEIGH BRILLIANT 1985.

POT-SHOTS NO. 3682.

WE ARE
LIVING
IN A WORLD
FULL
OF
UNPUNISHED
VILLAINS

AND
UNREWARDED
HEROES.

POT-SHOTS NO. 3621. Ashleigh Brilliant

THE GREATEST OBSTACLE TO DISCOVERING THE TRUTH

IS BEING CONVINCED THAT YOU ALREADY KNOW IT.

©ASHLEIGH BRILLIANT 1985

©ASHLEIGH BRILLIANT 1985.　　POT-SHOTS NO. 3839

SHAME ON OUR OPPONENTS

FOR USING THE SAME DESPICABLE METHODS WE OURSELVES HAVE ALWAYS USED WHEN NECESSARY.

Ashleigh Brilliant

©ASHLEIGH BRILLIANT 1985.　　POT-SHOTS NO. 3567.

I WANT WHAT MONEY CAN'T BUY ~

MORE MONEY.

Ashleigh Brilliant

February 14

February 15

February 16

POT-SHOTS NO. 3774.   Ashleigh Brilliant

Nobody
has yet
disputed
my claim
to be
the longest
surviving
victim
of your
neglect.

© ASHLEIGH BRILLIANT 1985.

February 17

© ASHLEIGH BRILLIANT 1985.   POT-SHOTS NO. 3865.

AFTER READING
SO MANY
"HOW-TO" BOOKS,

I'VE BECOME
AN EXPERT
ON HOW TO
SIT AND READ.

Ashleigh Brilliant

February 18

© ASHLEIGH BRILLIANT 1985.   Ashleigh Brilliant   POT-SHOTS NO. 3554.

CAUTION:
READ NO FURTHER
IF YOU ARE
EASILY OFFENDED.

THANKS FOR CONFIRMING
WHAT I SUSPECTED
ABOUT YOU.

February 22

February 23

February 24

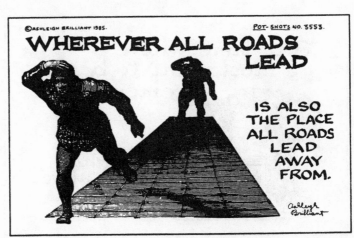

POT-SHOTS NO. 4268.

ONE THING AT LEAST IS CERTAIN ABOUT THE UNEXPECTED:

IT'S NEVER WHAT YOU EXPECT.

©ASHLEIGH BRILLIANT 1987.

Ashleigh Brilliant

©ASHLEIGH BRILLIANT 1985.

POT-SHOTS NO. 3869.

MY ONLY HOPE LIES IN YOUR NEVER FINDING OUT HOW MUCH I REALLY NEED YOU.

Ashleigh Brilliant

©ASHLEIGH BRILLIANT 1985.

POT-SHOTS NO. 3593.

The time when I most want to be remembered

is while I'm alive.

Ashleigh Brilliant

By ASHLEIGH BRILLIANT

POT-SHOTS NO. 4297

IT'S NEVER SHAMEFUL TO SEEK CONFIDENTIAL HELP,

EVEN IF YOUR REASON FOR NEEDING IT IS UTTERLY SHOCKING.

Ashleigh Brilliant

After All

I hope it has been a good year for you, and that our relationship has, if anything, been strengthened by travelling together all the way around the sun. Assuming that it has, or at least that we are still on speaking terms, you may (I hope) like to know where more of this good stuff can be had. If you can't find it (or enough of it) anywhere else, I invite you to establish your own direct line of communication with the source.

Here at Ashleigh Brilliant world headquarters (founded in 1967) we offer a unique mail-order system by which you have access to thousands of different messages, all available on postcards, and many in other exciting forms, including this series of books. Of course we guarantee satisfaction, and can, if necessary, overwhelm you with evidence that we usually provide it.

In addition, please consider me open to receive proposals for licensed uses of my Pot-Shots material, on products, or in other publications or media. Pot-Shots are available as a syndicated newspaper feature, and if I'm not already in your local paper, the responsibility is at least as much yours as it is mine.

I am also to some extent (and only while alive) available to make personal appearances, and would probably be more interested than you expect to receive your offer.

Whatever your specific interest, a pleasant way to begin extending our connection is by sending for my Catalogue. It comes with sample postcards and an enchanting order-form. The current (1987) price is Two U.S. Dollars. Please enclose that amount, or its equivalent in your own time and currency. My address is:

> Ashleigh Brilliant
> 117 W. Valerio St.
> Santa Barbara, California 93101, U.S.A.

POT-SHOTS NO. 4113.

POWERFUL
AS IT IS,
EVEN PRAYER
CAN HAVE
VERY LITTLE
EFFECT
ON
WHAT HAS
ALREADY
HAPPENED.

Ashleigh Brilliant

Appendix:
Calling all Collectors

Of the many products licensed by Ashleigh Brilliant, the following nine should be of particular interest to collectors, being no longer in production (and some of the manufacturers no longer in business). If you own any of these items, we recommend that you keep them in a safe place. There is no telling how much they may eventually be worth:

1. Ashleigh Brilliant's PICK-A-DILLY SQUARES (12 Novelty greeting-cards, foldable, with great difficulty, into colorful but absurdly non-functional little boxes. Aviva Enterprises, San Francisco, 1971.)

2. POT-SHOTS CAPS (24 messages, including #58, DON'T COME ANY CLOSER—I MIGHT LOVE YOU," in same format as syndicated newspaper feature. Paulison Co., Denver, 1981.)

3. POT-SHOTS "Little Messengers That Stand Up For You." (20 messages on nine-inch cardboard dolls standing in detachable wooden bases. Freelance Inc., Lansdale Pennsylvania, 1976.)

4. POT-SHOT APRONS (6 Vinyl-coated aprons with elaborate mock-classical motifs and Pot-Shot messages, some of which—contrary to our usual policy—were written specially for this product, e.g. "BLESSED ARE THE WASHERS-UP, FOR THEY SHALL INHERIT THE LEFTOVERS." United Notions Designs Ltd., Tunbridge Wells, England, 1982.)

5. BRILLIANT ANIMALS CALENDARS (Animal photographs matched with Pot-Shots. E.g., two amorous pigs with #105, "DO YOU MIND IF I APPRECIATE YOU?" Argus Communications, Allen, Texas, 1983 and 1984.)

6. BRILLIANT THOUGHTS NEEDLEPOINT KITS (11 messages with canvas, yarn, chart, needle, and supposedly "easy directions." Johnson Creative Arts Inc., West Townsend, Mass., 1983.)

7. BRILLIANT THOUGHTS MUGS (12 messages, gift-boxed, with a "personal" note from Ashleigh Brilliant expressing pleasure that, being ceramic, these inscriptions may endure to baffle future archaeologists. H. Dodge & Son Inc., Sylmar, California, 1984.)

8. ASHLEIGH BRILLIANT COCKTAIL NAPKINS (5 Pot-Shots were used, including #372, "IF ONLY I WERE HAVING AS MUCH FUN AS YOU PROBABLY THINK I AM." Monogram of California, San Francisco, 1978.)

9. ASHLEIGH BRILLIANT'S HALLMARK CARDS (Four greeting-cards—"Contemporary Cards" #75KF 705-2, 75KF 55-2, & 90KF 2-1, and "Note-Card" #BM638-4—using a total of 44 words, for which the author received $15,000, thus becoming the highest-paid writer, per word, in recorded history. Hallmark Cards Inc., Kansas City, Missouri, 1983.)

Select Bibliography

I. *Books and Articles Referring to Ashleigh Brilliant and His Works:*

Abraham, Matt. "The T-Shirt Philosopher," *The Advertiser* (Adelaide, Australia), Nov. 28, 1981.

Avery, Pamela. "The 'Brilliants' of a Syndicated Cartoonist," *Rocky Mountain News* (Denver), Feb. 15, 1979.

Berman, Laura. "Some Brilliant Pot-Shots at Life," *Detroit Free Press,* Feb. 8, 1979.

Blum, Walter. "Ashbury's Ash," *San Francisco Examiner,* June 9, 1968.

Boquist, Faye. "Pot-Shots Exude Life's True Ways," *San Jose News,* April 15, 1975.

Bowden, Jane A., ed., *Contemporary Authors,* Vol. 65–68. Detroit: Gale Research Co., 1977, p. 79.

Brandon, Brandy. "The Pulitzer Prize in Seventeen Words?" *California Senior Magazine,* March, 1987, pp. 10–11.

Brantingham, Barney. "Off The Beat" [report on Ashleigh Brilliant's winning Grand Prize in the Chiquita Banana Song Lyric Writing Contest], *Santa Barbara News-Press,* Oct. 1, 1986.

Caen, Herb. Column in *San Francisco Chronicle,* Aug. 2, 1967; July 29, 1970; Jan. 26, 1971; Nov. 21, 1974; Nov. 28, 1975; July 29, 1976; March 23, 1978; Dec. 21, 1982.

California Magazine. "Brilliant Deduction," Nov., 1984, p. 80.

Carpinteria (Calif.) *Herald.* "Herald's Brilliant Move Launches Cartoonist's Career," Jan. 21, 1986.

Carter, Lloyd G. "Author Seeks The Point Of Life," *Los Angeles Times* (from United Press International), Jan. 29, 1984.

Chatfield-Taylor, Joan. "Ashleigh Is Brilliant In 17 Words Or Less," *San Francisco Chronicle,* Oct. 30, 1979.

Conran, Shirley. "Psychological Postcards," *Vanity Fair* (London), March, 1972.

Cool, Margaret. "Those Pithy Pot-Shots," *Santa Barbara Magazine,* Summer, 1980.

Cooper, Candy. "Brilliant Ashleigh Takes Pot-Shots At Himself," *Independent Press-Telegram* (Long Beach, Calif.), July 2, 1980.

DeFlitch, Gerard. "Ashleigh Brilliant: Taking Pot-Shots At Life," Greensburg (Pennsylvania) *Tribune-Review,* May 10, 1987.

Denerstein, Robert. "Ashleigh Brilliant: A Billboard For Own Work," *Rocky Mountain News* (Denver), April 25, 1980.

Dewey, Jackie, R. N. "Brilliant Wit And Wisdom: Burnout Antidote," *Health Care Horizons* (San Pedro, Calif.), March 29, 1981.

Downey, Bill. "Brevity May Be Top Contribution Of Those Brilliant Pot-Shots," *Santa Barbara News-Press,* Nov. 26, 1978.

Godwin, John, Beth Bryant, and Rena Bulkin. *Arthur Frommer's Guide to San Francisco.* New York: Frommer/Pasmontier, 1977, p. 122.

Goldwag, William J., M.D. "A Time For Cheer," *Bestways,* Dec., 1984, p. 10.

Griscom, Elane. "Ashleigh Reviews His Brilliant Career," *Santa Barbara News-Press,* April 25, 1985.

Guernsey, John. "Firing Of Professor Raises Questions: Action Stirs Campus In Bend," *The Sunday Oregonian* (Portland), March 28, 1965.

Gustaitis, Rasa. *Turning On.* New York: Signet, 1969, pp. 200–201.

Helfand, Jerry. "Spicy Pot-Shots Banned In New York," *Santa Barbara News and Review,* July 12, 1979.

Hofstadter, Douglas R. *Metamagical Themas: Questing for the Essence of Mind and Pattern,* New York: Basic Books, 1985, pp. 47, 732, 803.

Holcombe, Chet. "New Milestone for 'Pot Shots' " [publication of Pot-Shot #1000], *Santa Barbara News-Press,* July 20, 1976.

Hopper, Ila Grant. "Ashleigh Brilliant Rides Again, Evens Score," Aug. 21, 1976. "Life's Just A Big Pot-Shot," July 21, 1985. *The Bulletin* (Bend, Oregon).

Impressions: The Magazine for the Imprinted Sportswear Industry. "The Law: *Brilliant vs. W. B. Productions:* Re-defining What Can And Can't Be Copyrighted," Feb., 1980, pp. 146–152.

Jackson, Beverley. "Ashleigh's Cards Brilliant," *Santa Barbara News-Press,* Dec. 9, 1973.

Joseph, Tony. "Bon Mots: Epigraphologist Likes To Make Brilliant Points," Ventura County (California) *Star-Free Press,* Jan. 7, 1986.

Korn, Eric. "Remainders" column, *The Times Literary Supplement* (London), March 20, 1987, p. 296.

Lillington, Karlin J. "The 17-Words-Or-Less World Of Ashleigh Brilliant," *Daily Nexus* (University of California at Santa Barbara), May 23, 1980.

Malan, Andre. "Needled By The Haystacks," *The West Australian* (Perth), Feb. 10, 1973. [Ashleigh Brilliant's one-man protest demonstration against a Perth band's amplified music.]

Moya, Mimi. " 'Pot-Shots' Begins Today," *The Record-Eagle* (Traverse City, Michigan), Dec. 31, 1984.

Mulvihill, Kathleen A. "Witty Words: Great Writing Can Be Brief . . . ," *The Times-Picayune/States Item* (New Orleans), May 25, 1981.

Neimark, Jill. "Absolutely Brilliant," *American Way* (magazine of American Airlines), Dec. 10, 1985, pp. 42–44.

Nelson, Roy Paul. *Cartooning.* Chicago: Henry Regnery, 1975, p. 43.

New Zealand Herald (Auckland). "New Cartoon Series Begins Today," March 31, 1973.

Orange County Illustrated (Santa Ana, California). "At Palm And Olive," Nov., 1966. [How Ashleigh Brilliant secured a free supply of Palmolive soap for the students of Chapman College's Floating University, whose headquarters happened to be at the corner of *Palm* and *Olive* Streets in Orange, California.]

Pattee, Sarah. "Pop Philosopher Reflects His Name," *San Diego Tribune,* Feb. 13, 1987.

Perlman, Martin. "Ashleigh Brilliant, Wise Guy," *Santa Barbara Independent,* Dec. 10, 1986, p. 23.

Perry, Charles. *The Haight-Ashbury: A History.* New York: Random House, 1984, p. 297.

Perry, Jenny. "Brilliant May Help Open Dispute Resolution Center," *Santa Barbara News-Press,* July 11, 1980.

Phillips, Bill. "Russian Club Achieves Campus Recognition: Brilliant Praises Council Action," *Spartan Daily* (San Jose State College, California), Oct. 23, 1958.

Richmond. "Erstwhile Bournemouth Schoolboy Makes His Fortune In America," *Evening Echo* (Bournemouth, England), May 25, 1971.

Ritter, Carl. "This Group Unified By Diversity," *San Diego Union,* May 30, 1976. [Ashleigh Brilliant and the Mensa Society.]

Santa Barbara News-Press. "Cartoonist May Sell Patty Note," Oct. 30, 1975. [How a letter from Patty Hearst to Ashleigh Brilliant was offered at auction by the New York autograph firm of Charles Hamilton.] "Local Cartoonist Claims Pay Record In Card Contract," July 10, 1984.

Santa Barbara News and Review. "Pot-Shots By Crafts Board: Ashleigh's License Axed," Nov. 19, 1976. [Ashleigh Brilliant forbidden to exhibit in local art show because his art contained words.]

Santa Barbara News and Review. "Unpredictable Independents Could Swing City Elections," Feb. 25, 1977. [Running for City Council.]

Santa Barbara Visitor Press. "Ashleigh Brilliant: The Father of Pot-Shots," July 3–10, 1986, p. 5.

Scarpinato, Mary. "Hoping To Hit The Target," *St. Louis Globe-Democrat,* April 19, 1975.

Shapiro, Saul. "Brilliant Lives Up To Name," *The Blade-Tribune* (Oceanside, California), June 6, 1976.

Showstack, Jonathan. "A Dime For Your Thoughts: How A Former B of A Teller Parlayed His One-Line Pot Shots Into A Postcard Empire," *The Bankamerican* (magazine of the Bank of America), May 1974.

Sligo Champion (Ireland). "Brilliant Sligo," Nov. 7, 1986.

Sun-Herald (Sydney, Australia). "Scholarly Funny-Man," Jan. 14, 1973.

Thrapp, Dan L. "Postcard Poetry," *Los Angeles Times,* Jan. 12, 1974.

Times-Star (Alameda, Calif.). "Oakland Museum Picks Associate Curator," Sept. 15, 1970.

Upland News (Upland, Calif.). "Likes It Here," Jan. 17, 1957.

Von Hoffman, Nicholas. *We Are the People Our Parents Warned Us Against.* New York: Fawcett, 1968, pp. 10–12.

Who's Who in the West. Chicago: Marquis, 1977—.

Woman's Day (Australia). "Dr. Brilliant's Tonic," May 20, 1974.

II *Books and Articles in Which (by Special Permission) Pot-Shots Are Quoted or Reproduced as Illustrations:*

Adler, Ronald B., and Neil Towne. *Looking Out/Looking In: Interpersonal Communication.* New York: Holt, Rinehart and Winston, 1987.

Block Petrella Weisbord/Designed Learning, Inc. *Staff Consulting Skills.* Plainfield, New Jersey, 1985.

Brown, Mark, and Julius Laffal. *Coping With Mental Disturbance.* Middletown, Ct.: Dept. of Psychology, Connecticut Valley Hospital, 1983.

The Busiest Bee (official publication of Mr. Bee Pollen Products). Scottsdale, Arizona: 1987–.

Cooke, Ann and Frank. *Cooking with Music.* Santa Barbara: Fiesta City Publishers, 1983.

Doty, Betty, and Pat Rooney. *The Anger Puzzle.* Redding, California: The Bookery Publishing Co., 1986.

Edward Hospital Women's Center For Health, Naperville Illinois. *Growing Pains . . . and Pleasures: A Program for Seventh Grade Girls.* 1985.

Evans, Terence T., (U.S. District Judge, Eastern District of Wisconsin). "Decision and Order in the Case of *Count Fuller, A/K/A Jeffrey Pergoli v. The Fuller Brush Co.*" Civil Action no. 83-C-592, Oct. 20, 1984.

Giegold, William C. *Management by Objectives.* New York: McGraw-Hilll, 1978.

Goleman, Daniel, Trygg Engen, and Anthony Davids. *Introductory Psychology.* New York: Random House, 1982.

Goodman, Joel (ed.). *Laughing Matters,* vol. 3, no. 2, Saratoga Institute, Saratoga Springs, N.Y., 1985.

Hayward, Susan. *A Guide for the Advanced Soul.* Spit Junction, NSW, Australia: In-Tune Books, 1984.

Heinich, Robert, Michael Molenda, and James D. Russell. *Instructional Media.* New York: John Wiley & Sons, 1982.

Houdart, Francoise. *People* (1974) and *Meeting People* (1982). Paris: Hatier. [A French text-book series for teaching English.]

Jackson County Juvenile Court. *The Open Line* (newsletter), Kansas City, Missouri, 1986–.

Kouri, Mary K. *Elderlife: A Time to Give—A Time to Receive.* Denver: Human Growth & Development Associates, 1985.

Lamb, Charles W. "A Space And A Witness," *Pilgrimage* [Journal of Psychotherapy and Personal Exploration], vol. 11, no. 2, Summer, 1983, pp. 68–78. "A Field Guide to Neurotic Behavior." *Pilgrimage*, vol. 12, no. 6, Nov./Dec., 1986, pp. 19–23.

Leong, Lim Chong. "My Child Is Smart," *Grow* [magazine for parents and teachers], Republic of Singapore, Ministry of Education, April, 1980.

Mosak, Harold H. *Ha Ha and Aha: The Role of Humor in Psychotherapy.* Muncie, Indiana: Accelerated Development Inc., 1987.

New South Wales Board of Senior School Studies. *Modern History: Specimen Examination Papers.* Sydney, Australia: 1986.

Pelton, Ross. *Mind Food and Smart Pills: How to Increase Your Intelligence and Prevent Brain Aging.* San Diego: T & R Publishers, 1986.

Reader's Digest. Feb., 1980, p. 242. Sept., 1982, p. 70. July, 1987, p. 144. In "Quotable Quotes," June, 1980 (inside front cover), July, 1983, p. 157.

Santa Barbara Trust for Historic Preservation. *La Campana*, 1984–.

Schaie, K. Warner, and James Geiwitz. *Adult Development and Aging.* Boston: Little, Brown, 1982.

Shapiro, Deane H., Jr. *Precision Nirvana.* Englewood Cliffs, N.J.: Prentice-Hall, 1978.

Short, Robert L. *A Time to be Born—A Time to Die.* New York: Harper, Row, 1973. [Pot-Shots matched with passages from the Book of Ecclesiastes.]

Swan, Michael. *Kaleidoscope.* Cambridge: Cambridge University Press, 1979. [An anthology of English for non-native speakers.]

Travis, John, M.D. *Wellness Workbook.* Mill Valley, Calif.: Wellness Resource Center, 1979.

Vailable, Ima. *San Diego Connections: The Complete Guide to Meeting the Opposite Sex in the 80's.* San Diego: Rathbone Unlimited, 1985.

Venture Inward [magazine of the Association for Research and Enlightenment], 1984–.

Watts, Dale. *The Romantic and Sensualist's Guide to the San Francisco Bay Area.* Oakland, Calif.: Hart-Eden Press, 1986.

Young, David P. *21st Century Pioneering: A Scrapbook of the Future.* New York: Friendship Press, 1986.